What's So HOT About VOLCANOES?

WENDELL A. DUFFIELD

Illustrations by Bronze Black

2011
Mountain Press Publishing Company
Missoula, Montana

Cover Photo: *An eruption at the Mauna Ulu vent of Kilauea Volcano in 1969. The fountain was about 2,000 feet tall. As the lava fell back to Earth, it flowed into channels leading to a deep crater. The steam in the foreground was created by rain falling on a hot lava surface.*

Back Cover Photo: *Villarrica Volcano in the Andes Mountains of Chili during a mild eruption in 1977.*

Photos © 2011 by Wendell A. Duffield unless otherwise credited
Illustrations © 2011 by Bronze Black unless otherwise credited

**Other books in the *What's So Cool About Geology?* series
WHAT'S SO GREAT ABOUT GRANITE?**

WHAT'S SO COOL ABOUT GEOLOGY?
is a registered trademark of
Mountain Press Publishing Company

Library of Congress Cataloging-in-Publication Data

Duffield, Wendell A.
  What's so hot about volcanoes? / Wendell A. Duffield ; illustrations by Bronze Black.
    p. cm.
  Includes bibliographical references and index.
  ISBN 978-0-87842-574-7 (pbk. : alk. paper)
  1. Volcanoes—Juvenile literature. 2. Volcanism—Juvenile literature. I. Black, Bronze, ill. II. Title.
QE521.3.D847 2011
551.21—dc23
                        2011013689

PRINTED IN HONG KONG

MP Mountain Press
PUBLISHING COMPANY
P.O. Box 2399 • Missoula, MT 59806 • 406-728-1900
800-234-5308 • info@mtnpress.com
www.mountain-press.com

To Marlowe "Red" Severson, the best teacher I had during my twenty years of formal schooling.

THANK-YOUS

Several colleagues have graciously allowed me to use their photographs in this book. Their names appear in the photo credits. Volcanologist Bob Tilling critiqued the entire draft manuscript, improving style and content. Colleagues Nancy Riggs and Michael Ort served as sounding boards for questions that arose as I wrote. The final prepublication editing at Mountain Press by Jennifer Carey, as well as freelance copy-editor Jasmine Star, added more professional polish.

The inspiration for writing this book is fondly credited to the many enthusiastic students and their teachers from classrooms I've visited to talk about volcanoes during the past four-plus decades, and who have been with me on many field trips. Their interest, appreciation, and eagerness to learn are what set me on track to start writing a book about volcanoes for younger folks, eventually leading to the publication of the book you hold in your hands. So, I credit and heartily thank the students in my life for making this book happen.

I also thank my wife, Anne, for allowing me to repeatedly, though always briefly, put our life together on hold during the times I disappeared to be with students and teachers, and for understanding why I hung the "Do Not Disturb" sign on my office door while writing this book.

CONTENTS

Thank-Yous   iv

Heating Up   1

What's So Hot About Volcanoes?   5
Earth's Internal Heater   9
Blowing Off Steam   10

Where Do Volcanoes Form?   13
Volcanoes at Plate Collision Zones   13
Volcanoes at Spreading Zones   18
Volcanoes at Sliding Boundaries   20
Volcanoes Far from Plate Boundaries   21

Why Does Some Magma Flow and Some Magma Blow?   27
THE FAMILY OF VOLCANOES   30
Cinder Cones   31
Shield Volcanoes   34
Flood Basalts   35
Stratovolcanoes   38
Lava Domes   42
Violent Caldera-Forming Pyroclastic Eruptions   46

What Happens When Molten Rock Meets Water?   57
When Magma Meets Groundwater   57
When Lava Meets Surface Water   60

Can Eruptions Be Predicted?   63

Are Volcanoes Our Friends or Enemies?   67

Cooling Down   74

Where to Explore Young Volcanoes in the United States   79

Glossary   81

Resources   85

Index   86

A 2,000-degree-Fahrenheit lava flow moves along Chain of Craters Road near Mauna Ulu on Kilauea Volcano's east flank in 1970.

HEATING UP

I parked the jeep at the abrupt new end of the road where a lava flow had buried the pavement only a week earlier. I retrieved my gear-filled backpack and a two-way radio from the passenger seat and hiked onto the black lava. It was so young it was still warm to the touch, and the bright tropical sunshine added extra heat. The surface sparkled like freshly broken glass. In fact, it was glass—volcanic glass, a brittle kind of rock that forms when molten lava cools and solidifies too fast for crystals to grow. The glass crackled underfoot with each step I took. A gentle breeze carried the lava's sulfurous scent of rotten eggs.

Five minutes and a couple hundred yards later, I stopped near the far edge of the flow. I turned and looked back across the shiny black expanse to the jeep. Lush tropical forest that had escaped the new lava lay behind me. The trees were alive with the chirping of birds hidden within their leafy camouflage.

I was the newest member, the two-month rookie, on a team of a dozen scientists and technicians studying Kilauea, one of the world's most active volcanoes. Our office was the Hawaiian Volcano Observatory on the Big Island of Hawaii. The team's main goal was to understand Kilauea's behavior well enough that we could warn people living nearby if an eruption seemed imminent.

The director of the observatory had sent me down the east side of Kilauea to inspect an area we thought might be building toward an eruption. Today's task was to find out what was happening not far beneath my feet. I dropped my backpack on the lava. Except for the songs of the bird choir, all seemed quiet.

I drew the two-way radio from its holster and pushed the send button to call the staff seismologist at the observatory, about 10 miles away at the top of Kilauea.

"Observatory. Observatory. This is Duff calling Bob. Duff calling Bob. Over."

A few seconds later I heard, "Yeah, Duff. This is Bob. What's up?"

"I'm down near Mauna Ulu, scouting around on the newest lava flow, like the boss asked me to." I paced around on the lava as I talked. "I don't see anything unusual. The place looks like it did yesterday and several days before that. Nothing's really changed since the road got buried." A pause suggested that Bob was mulling over his answer.

"Actually, Duff, I was about to call you. I'm here watching our seismic recorders, and I'm seeing the tracings of small quakes—hundreds of them. This started a couple minutes ago. It looks like the shaking is coming from under right about where I think you might be."

My heart started to beat faster, energized by a mixture of excitement and fear.

"The tracings tell me the depth where the shaking originates is shallow and getting closer to the surface by the minute," Bob continued. "But I don't think you'd feel anything unless you're right over the restless spot."

Even though I was a rookie, I had already learned enough from the volcano veterans to know that swarms of small quakes rising up through the ground usually meant that magma, or underground molten rock, was forcing its way toward the surface. It was breaking and pushing solid rock aside, creating earthquakes as it rose.

"You might want to get away from that area with the newest lava," Bob cautioned.

Couldn't agree more, I thought. "Yeah. Will do."

But first I closed my eyes and stood as still as possible to test something I'd been told about by the old-timers. I felt it! Barely, but it was there. The ground and I were trembling. It was a gentle shake, and I knew it wasn't from wind or tired legs. I also thought I felt an occasional sharp jerk of the ground. Bob and other earthquake experts who study volcanoes call the steady shaking volcanic tremor. Tremor together with small earthquakes is almost a sure sign that magma is on the move. I got on the radio again.

Lava peeks out of new 1-foot-wide crack near Mauna Ulu in 1970.

Lava erupting from a crack at Kilauea Volcano. This lava fountain is about 300 feet long and up to 50 feet high. This type of eruption is often called a curtain of fire, *even though there is no fire, only the fiery red color of the lava.*

"Hey, Bob. I feel what I think is tremor. I'm heading back to the car."

"I see tremor in the tracings here now," he said. "Get moving!"

I shoved the radio into its holster and stooped over to pick up my backpack. As I straightened up, I saw something incredible. A new crack was slowly opening across the lava, and the leading edge was moving straight toward me. It was still about 100 feet away. As the crack widened from a hair's width to several inches and then more, the air above it began to swirl in turbulent heat waves, like the air above desert sand or a paved road does on a hot summer day.

I quickly fished the camera out of my backpack and snapped a few pictures as a bright red bulb of molten lava, about the size of a football, began to slowly ooze out. It looked like a gopher peeking from his underground home to check for threats before completely emerging. Then other headlike bulbs began to appear, as though all the molten gophers of Hawaii were about to gather for a convention. I didn't want any part of that party. Neither did the birds. They stopped singing and flew away to safer trees.

I ran to the jeep. When I looked back, I saw a long blade of molten lava knifing 30 feet upward from the crack and splashing back to the ground. I was the sole human audience for this curtain of fire—an eruption of lava from a deep crack in the ground.

Wow, I thought. I'm getting paid to do this!

3

This two-step cascade of lava is spilling into 540-foot-deep Alae Crater at Kilauea in 1969. The crater was filled with lava within a few months and is no longer visible. —PHOTO COURTESY OF DON SWANSON, U.S. GEOLOGICAL SURVEY

What's So HOT About VOLCANOES?

Volcanoes, those living mountains that belch forth hot stinky fumes, gritty ash, and molten rock, have mesmerized and terrified humans for centuries. Volcanoes have been around throughout Earth's history—much longer than people—and we humans must adjust our lives to this sizzling force of nature or pay a price. And although payment may be in the form of lost life and property, people continue to live on and near volcanoes in order to take advantage of their rich agricultural soils, abundant construction materials, valuable green energy resources, and inspiration for a variety of artistic pursuits. Yet people who are attracted to volcanoes should remember one sure truth: A volcano that seems to be in safe slumber has at some time been fiery hot. And that fire may not be out; it may just be temporarily hidden while the volcano is on a path to renewed eruption.

Volcanoes exist because the interior of Earth is very hot. The explanation for this heat begins with the formation of our planet about 4.55 billion years ago. When Earth was new it probably was a mostly molten ball—a bunch of rocky debris from within the solar system that gravity pulled together so forcefully that it melted. Late in Earth's period of formation, a chunk of material about the size of Mars crashed into the growing planet. Some material splashed back into space, where the force of gravity pulled it together to create the Moon. Scientist theorize that the collision was at an angle, instead of straight down, and tilted Earth's rotation axis enough to result in what we enjoy as spring, summer, winter, and fall. If Earth rotated on a vertical axis, life at any given latitude would not experience the annual seasonal changes. In theory, a big angular collision may also have set Earth spinning on its axis at a speed that we experience as a 24-hour day. It seems that the big wreck about 4.5 billion years ago set the stage for a lot of human life today.

Early Earth was so hot that the material inside it flowed around like the ingredients in a near-boiling pot of thick oatmeal. As the molten debris churned away, the different chemical ingredients started to sort themselves out by their densities, similar to the processes that cause a rock to sink in water while wood floats.

Most of the heaviest material sank and collected at or near the center of the planet. Lighter materials stayed higher up, closer to the surface, creating a layered ball. The lightest substances—water and air—rose toward the top to form the two outermost layers, the oceans and the atmosphere.

The material that eventually cooled enough to become the rocky part of the ball separated into three main layers: the core, the mantle, and the crust. In a three-dimensional cutaway view, it looks like a gigantic onion. The innermost part is the

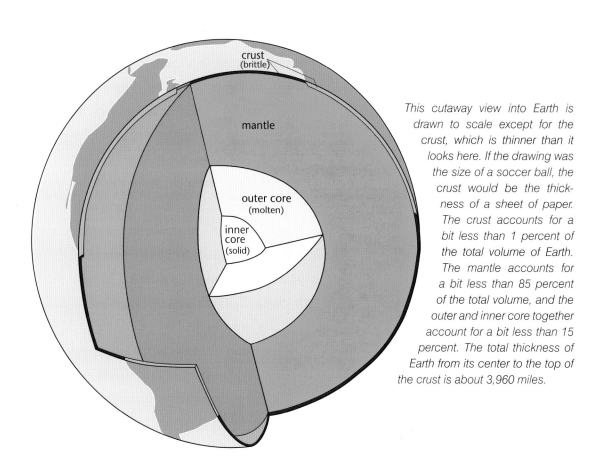

crust
(brittle)

mantle

outer core
(molten)

inner
core
(solid)

This cutaway view into Earth is drawn to scale except for the crust, which is thinner than it looks here. If the drawing was the size of a soccer ball, the crust would be the thickness of a sheet of paper. The crust accounts for a bit less than 1 percent of the total volume of Earth. The mantle accounts for a bit less than 85 percent of the total volume, and the outer and inner core together account for a bit less than 15 percent. The total thickness of Earth from its center to the top of the crust is about 3,960 miles.

core, which is mostly a mixture of the dense metals iron and nickel. Around that, the mantle is mostly made of heavy minerals rich in the elements silicon, oxygen, iron, magnesium, and calcium. The crust, the outermost rocky layer, is like a thin coat of frosting. It originally contained mostly less-dense silicate minerals rich in sodium and potassium that crystallized from molten material. Rocks that solidify from molten material are known as *igneous*, and the crust of early Earth was entirely igneous rock. Over the long expanses of geologic time, erosion of the igneous rock generated sediment that was deposited in layers, becoming what's known as *sedimentary rock*. Heat and pressure transformed some of the igneous and sedimentary rocks into new forms; these altered rocks are known as *metamorphic rocks.*

Even after 4.55 billion years, the Earth's separation into the three main layers isn't perfect. Some of the lighter material is still mixed with the heavy stuff deep down. And some of the heavy material remains higher up in the crust. It's harder for materials to move and separate by density now because the planet is cooler these days, so the Earth is more solid and dense.

Cooler, yes, but the temperature of the inner part of the core is thought to be somewhere in the range of 9,000 to 11,000 degrees Fahrenheit. That's hot enough to still be molten, if only the pressure of all the layers pushing down on it wasn't so high. One way that molten rock becomes solid is when the pressure on it is increased, even without lowering the temperature. So the inner part of the core is solid, but the outer part is molten. Scientists know this because a certain type of earthquake wave that can't pass through liquids can't pass through this part of the core. The outer core would be solid, like the inner core, except that there's less pressure on it because there's less material pushing on it from above.

Temperature decreases from the core toward Earth's surface. Across the mantle, it stays close to hot enough to melt the rocks. Even high up in the crust, just a couple thousand feet below Earth's surface, the temperature is still more than 100 degrees Fahrenheit. The work of deep-underground miners is a sweaty job.

The bottom line is that it's still hot enough inside Earth that some of the mantle rocks melt from time to time, forming magma. And some of that magma rises to the surface to create volcanoes. These days the number of volcanoes that erupt above sea level during a typical year is probably between fifty and one hundred, according to records compiled during the past fifty years. More volcanoes may have erupted in the past, when Earth was hotter.

Sarychev Volcano, in the Kuril Islands of Russia, erupting on June 12, 2009. The rising brown column of hot ash has punched a circular hole in the white cloud cover. It also pushed up moist air from a lower and warmer level of the atmosphere. At the higher and cooler level above the ash column, the moisture in that air has condensed to a cap of white steam. At ground level, turbulent clouds of white and dark brown volcanic debris flow down the sides of the volcano. Photo taken from the International Space Station, 200 miles above Earth's surface. —PHOTO COURTESY OF NASA

WHEN IS LAVA NOT MAGMA?

Melted rock is called *magma* when it's under the ground. Magma originates deep within the Earth and rises buoyantly to the surface like a cork in water—but not nearly as fast. Magma erupts through a volcanic vent, a fracture in Earth's crust through which magma can flow. Vents range from steep pipelike passageways to long cracks. Once at the surface, magma is called *lava.* It may seem like an odd distinction, but the conditions deep within Earth are much different than conditions at the surface, so the behavior of molten rock changes once it exits the vent of a volcano. That's one reason why it's good to have separate names for the two types of melted rock. When molten lava cools and becomes solid, that rock is also called *lava.*

A lava dome (the light-colored, vegetation-free mountaintop) grows at Soufrière Hills Volcano on the Caribbean island of Montserrat in 1998. Noxious white fumes rise from the top of the dome. Loose dome rocks have tumbled down the steep mountainside to build a delta into the Caribbean Sea. —PHOTO COURTESY OF RICK HOBLITT, U.S. GEOLOGICAL SURVEY

EARTH'S INTERNAL HEATER

Four and a half billion years seems like plenty of time for once-molten Earth to have become cold, solid rock, so why is the inside of Earth still hot? It probably would be cold and solid if not for radioactivity. Several of Earth's chemical elements occur in radioactive forms, called *isotopes*, which spontaneously change into other elements. Scientists call this process *decay*, and it releases a lot of heat. For example, heat from the decay of a radioactive isotope of uranium is used to boil water into high-pressure steam, which spins the turbine of a nuclear power plant, producing electricity.

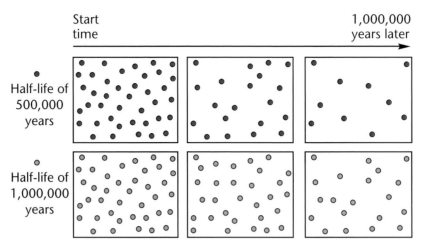

Half of the radioactive isotope represented by blue dots has decayed to stable, nonradioactive material in 1 million years. During the same period of time, three-fourths of the red isotope has decayed.

The amount of a radioactive isotope decreases by 50 percent during what is called its *half-life*. The half-lives of some isotopes are only minutes to hours long. Other half-lives are millions of years, and a few are even billions of years. Those with long half-lives, especially radioactive isotopes of uranium, thorium, and potassium, are the main sources of heat that help keep inner Earth's temperature high today.

When an object's heat energy is in balance with that of its surroundings, the two are said to have reached *thermal equilibrium*. Earth has been losing heat to outer space for 4.55 billion years and has not yet come to equilibrium with its neighborhood in the solar system. With its internal radioactive furnaces constantly generating new heat, Earth won't become a ball of cold stone any time soon.

BLOWING OFF STEAM

If Earth didn't have a way to get rid of its pent-up internal heat, it could blow its lid like an overheated sealed container of water. Volcanic eruptions are nature's version of this kind of blowout. They quickly spew lots of heat into the atmosphere when pressure has built up beyond the ability of Earth's lid, the crust, to hold the hot magma inside. Deep beneath the crust, though, where most of Earth's heat is stored, the heat rises to the surface far more slowly. This happens in two ways: conduction and convection.

When a piece of any hot solid material touches a second piece that's cooler, heat moves, or flows, from the warmer to the cooler solid until the two pieces reach the same temperature. This type of movement of heat is called *conduction*. Heat moves up from the depths of Earth and then across the crust in this way, and eventually dissipates into outer space. Heat conduction within the Earth is slow.

In the process known as *convection,* heat moves faster. In convection, a continuous loop of a flowing substance carries heat from a warmer to a cooler part of the loop during a cycle. Substances that are hotter are usually less dense, so convection occurs when a hot, less dense part of a substance rises buoyantly until it has cooled enough to be relatively dense. Then it sinks back down, where it gets reheated and rises again. The flowing substance moves in a huge loop called a *convection cell*. Over long periods of geologic time, the rocks of the mantle, which are always close to their melting temperature, flow in convection loops that transfer heat upward to the base of the crust.

But wait! If the mantle is rock, how can it flow? Given enough time at rest, many objects that people think of as being stiff and brittle solids can change shape without breaking. An increase in temperature increases the ability of many materials to change shape. If you could collect a chunk of hot rock from deep within the mantle and hit it with a heavy hammer, it would break into pieces as though it were cold and brittle. But over the long stretch of geologic time, that same hot rock sitting down inside the mantle can change shape and move without breaking, by c r e e p i n g s l o w l y   a l o n g like a thick, sticky syrup. Rocks have been made to behave this way in laboratory experiments that imitate the temperature and pressure conditions of the mantle.

Because the mantle makes up nearly 85 percent of Earth, the popular image of a fiery, swirling underworld isn't too far from the truth. The heat of Earth stirs up incredible unrest, making the mantle flow sluggishly in many convection loops over the long geologic haul. Some mantle material also flows slowly upward in wide pipe-like zones, called *mantle plumes*, heating the base of the crust at places called *hot spots*.

Earth's thin crust is so light and brittle that it floats on the mantle, moving around in response to the mantle's convection currents and mantle plumes.

Internal conduction and convection, as well as volcanic eruptions, are Earth's ways of getting rid of heat. Earth will continue to lose heat until the amount escaping from the planet is in balance with the amount coming in from the Sun.

Crested Pool, a boiling hot spring in Yellowstone National Park. The white material around the edge of the pool is sinter, deposited as the water cools.
—PHOTO COURTESY OF ROBERT O. FOURNIER, U.S. GEOLOGICAL SURVEY

SOAKING IN THE HEAT OF CONVECTION

Groundwater that occupies pore spaces and fractures within the Earth's crust moves by convection, too, but at a much faster speed than mantle rocks do. In addition to carrying heat upward, convecting groundwater also carries dissolved mineral salts. When the hot groundwater rises up, it becomes cooler, and at cooler temperatures it can't hold as many dissolved salts. So the salts may come out of solution to create mineral deposits in the upper (cooler) parts of a convection loop. If you've visited a hot spring, you've seen where the top of a groundwater convection loop leaks out onto Earth's surface. Deposits from the mineral-rich springwater can be either a delicately layered white rock called *travertine* (a form of calcium carbonate) or a white rock called *sinter* (a form of silica). Think twice about soaking in the heat of convection—some hot springs are literally boiling and many others will severely burn skin on contact.

Where Do VOLCANOES Form?

Internal, heat-driven turmoil over the course of Earth's long history has broken the thin, floating cap of brittle crust into huge slabs, called *plates*, that slide around atop the moving mantle. Each plate moves a couple of inches per year relative to its neighbors. Some movement occurs at a slow, steady pace, while other movement happens from time to time in quick jerks during powerful earthquakes. The plates dance around like a gigantic, slow-motion version of the patches of scum that skitter across the surface of a near-boiling pot of thick broth. The boundaries between plates are where most volcanoes occur.

There are fourteen principle plates and several small miniplates on Earth today. The total number has been different at times during the geologic past, and there will almost certainly be a new arrangement and a different number of plates in the geologic future. Plates consist of continents, ocean floors, or a combination of the two. Geologists call the dynamic system of these moving pieces *global plate tectonics*. There are three types of boundaries between plates: where plates collide, where they drift away from each other, and where they slide past each other.

VOLCANOES AT PLATE COLLISION ZONES

Where two ocean-floor plates collide head-on, one bends downward beneath the other and sinks into the mantle at a gentle to moderate angle, a bit like what happens when a shirttail is tucked into the waistband of jeans. The boundary where the colliding plates rub against each other—at and below Earth's surface—is called a *subduction zone*. Many earthquakes occur within subduction zones, to depths as much as 400 miles, as the leading edge of a "tucked" plate moves deeper and deeper into the mantle. Subduction zones also occur where an ocean-floor plate collides with a continent.

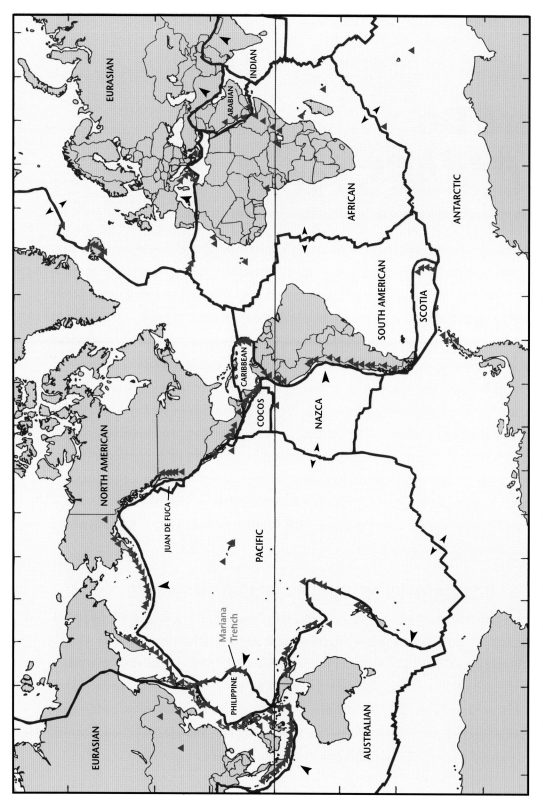

The names and outlines of Earth's tectonic plates. The black triangles point in the directions the plates move relative to each other. The heavy black lines are boundaries between plates. The red triangles mark locations of historically active volcanoes.

TECTONIC PLATES, CRUST, AND APPLE PIE

Long before geologists accepted plate tectonics as an explanation for the horizontal movements of Earth's surface, a geologist by the name of Andrija Mohorovicic discovered that the travel speed of earthquake waves abruptly decreases as they approach the surface. This change happens about 5 miles beneath ocean floors and 30 miles beneath continents. The boundary across which speed changes is called the Moho (or M-discontinuity) in honor of its discoverer. The slowdown happens when seismic waves move from heavy, dense rocks in the mantle to less dense rocks above. By definition, those less dense rocks above the Moho are Earth's crust.

Another boundary also affects the speed of earthquake waves. At about 62 miles below the surface, the travel speed of earthquake waves abruptly decreases as they move toward the interior of Earth. This slower zone extends downward another 100 miles and consists of mantle rocks that are hot enough to be soft and squishy—maybe even partly molten—rather than hard and brittle like the rocks above. This soft, squishy layer, called the *asthenosphere*, is where much of the convection in the mantle occurs. (*Asthenes* is Greek for "weak.") The brittle rocks above the asthenosphere, called the *lithosphere*, are what Earth's tectonic plates are made of. (*Lithos* is Greek for "rock.")

Technically speaking, tectonic plates are made of lithosphere: the crust (as defined by the Moho) plus the hard and brittle top part of the mantle. Many people describe tectonic plates as pieces of crust, rather than pieces of lithosphere. I think it's okay for people to talk about tectonic plates of crust because the words *crust* and *mantle* aren't tongue twisters, like *lithosphere* and *asthenosphere*. But keep in mind that the plates are actually pieces of lithosphere, which is both crust and upper mantle.

I like to think of the lithosphere as the crisp, brown crust on my mom's homemade apple pie, which breaks up into thin platy pieces when I cut into it with a fork. The gooey, sugary, apple-rich filling underneath is the asthenosphere of my dessert. Sometimes that soft stuff is so fluid that I need a spoon to scoop it into my mouth! Straight out of the oven, it's hot and runny and stays that way for a while. The crust is almost instantly cool and brittle.

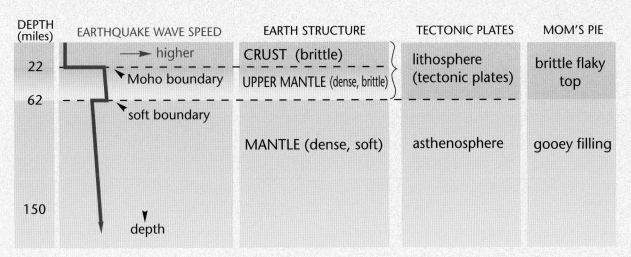

The speed of earthquake waves changes at depth within the Earth. The change happens because of an abrupt increase in rock density between the base of the crust and the top of the mantle, and an abrupt decrease in rock brittleness between the uppermost mantle and the hot, soft, deeper mantle.

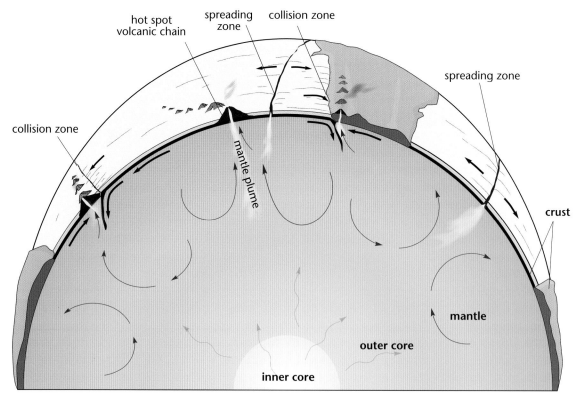

Heat flows outward from the core, generating convection in the mantle, spreading zones and collision zones in the crust, and mantle plumes that feed magma to hot spot volcanoes.

Because ocean-floor rocks are heavier than continental crust, ocean-floor plates always dive beneath continental plates. When two ocean-floor plates collide, the denser plate will dive beneath the lighter one. In either case, deep trenches form on the seafloor where an ocean-floor plate disappears beneath its neighbor. The deepest part of Earth's oceans is almost 7 miles below sea level in the Mariana Trench, where the Pacific Plate dives under the Philippine Plate.

The north and west sides of the Pacific Ocean are bounded by many long chains of islands that sit above subduction zones where an ocean plate is sliding beneath another ocean plate. These islands, including Japan and the Aleutians of Alaska, are made of volcanoes that have been built up from magma created in and above subduction zones. On the east side of the Pacific Ocean, where ocean-floor plates are sliding down beneath the edges of continents, volcanoes have formed on the continent above the subduction zone. These volcanoes form the Andes of South America, the volcanoes of central Mexico, and the Cascade Range of North America.

Water is a key ingredient for creating magma in a subduction zone. Because water helps break down the chemical bonds in minerals, adding water can cause a rock to start melting even without raising the temperature. In a subduction zone, the top part of the downgoing plate is water-saturated sediment on the seafloor and minerals that have water as one of their components. As this goopy mixture descends into the mantle, water is squeezed out and percolates upward, triggering the melting of mantle rock. Some of the subducting plate may melt, too. The magma rises buoyantly, erupting and building long chains of volcanoes.

Volcanoes don't occur where continents collide with each other. Because continents consist mostly of Earth's lightest rocks, they're like huge islands floating on the heavier mantle below. When two of these floating masses collide, neither one is heavy enough to sink into the mantle. Instead, they smash together in a slow-motion version of a head-on collision between freight trains. About 55 million years ago, a chunk of continent (called India today) rammed into another chunk (called Asia today). That collision began the incredible crunching, squeezing, folding, breaking, and lifting up of the two continental masses. This pile-up created the lofty Himalaya region, often called "the roof of the world" because of its high elevations. The top of

A GLOBAL BALANCING ACT

In spite of all the spreading and subducting and erupting, the size of Earth and its crust doesn't seem to grow or shrink. The amount of new crust created in spreading zones matches the amount of crust that disappears down into the mantle in subduction zones. That's an impressive balancing act!

Far into the geologic future, Earth will have cooled so much that tectonic plates will no longer move and volcanoes will not erupt. There won't be enough internal heat to drive these processes. By that distant future time, Earth will also be somewhat smaller because rocks shrink when they cool.

29,035-foot-tall Mount Everest, Earth's highest mountain, is capped by limestone, a sedimentary rock that originally formed on an ocean floor. It's had quite an upward ride, and the trip isn't over yet! But despite their massive size, Mount Everest and the other Himalayan mountains are not volcanoes.

VOLCANOES AT SPREADING ZONES

Where two plates move away from each other, the boundary is called a *spreading zone*. An excellent example zigzags its way up the middle of the Atlantic Ocean. The spreading there increases the distance between Africa and South America and between Europe and North America. When you look at a map of the world, it doesn't take much imagination to see that the continents on opposite sides of the Atlantic Ocean once fit together. In between, as the width of the ocean grows, volcanism along the spreading zone has created Iceland, and the country gets wider as spreading continues. The reason lava has piled up above sea level to create the island is because a mantle plume lies within the mid-Atlantic spreading zone under Iceland, adding extra magma for eruptions at this part of the spreading zone.

When two plates of crust move apart, the pressure on the mantle is reduced beneath the spreading zone. This release of pressure causes the mantle to start melting, and the magma moves into the spreading zone. It pushes up the crust above it, creating a ridge with a deep canyonlike crack down the middle. Magma erupts from the crack and adds lava, which solidifies into new rock along the trailing edges of each of the plates.

Because there are so many thousands of miles of spreading zones and because most are on the seafloor (except at Iceland and a small piece of northeast Africa), many volcanic eruptions happen there. The exact number isn't known because they're hidden beneath thousands of feet of water. But probably three-fourths of all Earth's volcanic eruptions occur on the seafloor.

About 75 percent of Earth is covered with oceans. The ocean floors consist of volcanic rocks erupted along spreading zones. The farther ocean-floor lava is from its source spreading zone, the older it is. With time, the once-new lava slowly gets covered with thin layers of dead sea plants and animals and with sediments washed

A 700-degree-Fahrenheit black smoker on the seafloor at a depth of 7,190 feet on the Juan de Fuca spreading zone, between the Juan de Fuca and Pacific Plates, off the coast of Oregon. The white and red growths are tube worms, which feed on chemicals, such as sulfides, emitted by the black smokers. The steel cylinders are about 3 feet long. They contain instruments that measure temperature and the amount of chemicals coming out of the black smokers. —PHOTO COURTESY OF WILLIAM CHADWICK, NATIONAL OCEANIC AND ATMOSPHERIC ADMINISTRATION VENTS PROGRAM

in by rivers and streams in coastal areas. Today, the most ancient ocean-floor lava is about 200 million years old and is located beneath the far western Pacific Ocean. All older ocean-floor lava has been tucked into subduction zones and returned to the mantle. Some of this material was melted to magma that fed volcanic eruptions above the subduction zones.

Lava flows of recent seafloor eruptions in spreading zones have been photographed by small submarine-like vessels during both manned and unmanned dives. These expeditions have also photographed chimney-shaped formations called *black smokers*. Water that's been heated by magma flows through these formations and deposits a variety of minerals when it mixes with cold seawater. Black smokers are the much hotter, deep-sea counterparts of hot springs at Earth's surface, releasing heat from inner Earth.

VOLCANOES AT SLIDING BOUNDARIES

The world-famous San Andreas Fault in California is an example of the third type of boundary between tectonic plates, where two plates slide past each other sideways. This type of movement, known as a *transform fault*, is slicing the state into two pieces. As the plates on opposite sides of the fault move, they're bringing San Francisco and Los Angeles closer to each other. But since they're moving just a couple of inches each year, these cities won't be neighbors any time soon.

View from the west of the San Andreas Fault in the Carrizo Plain area of southern California. The trace of the fault is the obvious trench that runs horizontally across the picture. Land on the far side is part of the North American Plate, and that on the near side is part of the Pacific Plate. The stream (Wallace Creek) once flowed straight across the fault but has been offset about 400 feet by movement along the fault. —PHOTO COURTESY OF MICHAEL COLLIER

For a demonstration of how this works, hold your hands out flat in front of you, index fingers against each other and thumbs tucked below. Now slide one hand toward your body while keeping the other hand still. The motion between your index fingers is like what happens along a transform fault. The plates move in parallel but opposite directions and remain in the same horizontal plane.

There are very few volcanoes along transform faults, probably because the parallel movement between plates doesn't allow water to move down into the mantle and also doesn't reduce the pressure on the mantle. However, exceptions may occur when the movement along the fault includes enough opening between plates to cause melting of the mantle due to pressure reduction. Examples include several volcanoes along the Dead Sea transform fault between Jordan and Israel.

VOLCANOES FAR FROM PLATE BOUNDARIES

Not all volcanoes occur along plate boundaries. Some erupt within plates at hot spots, places where mantle plumes rise up beneath the crust. The top of a plume starts to melt as it gets closer to the surface because pressure decreases as the thickness of rocks above decreases. The new magma rises to the surface and erupts.

The chain of Hawaiian Islands is a classic example of hot spot eruptions. This hot spot is beneath the central part of the Pacific Plate, in the middle of the Pacific Ocean. As the plate moves over the mantle plume, new volcanoes add links to the island chain. The youngest link is the island of Hawaii, popularly known as the Big Island. It has three active volcanoes: Mauna Loa, Hualalai, and Kilauea. Several miles to the southeast and still below sea level, an active volcano named Loihi needs to grow upward another 3,000 feet to see the light of day. The oldest link in this hot spot volcano chain formed about 80 million years ago and lies about 4,000 miles to the northwest. Most of the older links are no longer islands. They are ancient enough to have been eroded to a bit below sea level. Even though they don't extend above the sea, they're still large, impressive volcanic features.

Some volcanoes are on continents, far from the boundaries of plates. For example, several hundred volcanoes in northern Arizona lie within the North American Plate. Sunset Crater, the youngest, erupted about 1,000 years ago, destroying nearby homes of Native Americans.

MINIATURE PLATE TECTONICS AT KILAUEA VOLCANO

Earth's plates move so slowly that it's difficult for people to visualize the process of plate tectonics. In 1970, not long after the theory of plate tectonics had been proposed, Kilauea Volcano provided a small, fast-moving model that helped scientists understand the big picture. Back then, a 100- by 200-foot crater contained a deep lake of molten lava covered with a quarter- to half-inch-thick solid, black crust. (A thin solid layer always forms quickly on the surface of molten rock when it's chilled by contact with the atmosphere.) Beneath this crust, 2,000-degree-Fahrenheit lava churned, mimicking Earth's mantle. The brittle crust responded by breaking into pieces that moved relative to each other. Movements along the boundary zones between pieces were like the movements of Earth's tectonic plates.

Across a spreading zone, the plates of cooled lava moved away from each other at a speed of about 20 feet per minute—fast enough for an observer to easily see and accurately measure. At this speed, movements along mini transform faults were also obvious. At collision zones, one plate of lava slipped down beneath its neighbor, just like the big-picture process of subduction. The top plate sometimes folded and crumpled as the piece that was sliding beneath it pushed against it.

This 100- by 200-foot pool of molten lava (orange) that formed at the Mauna Ulu vent of Kilauea Volcano in 1970 is mostly covered by a thin black crust. The narrow orange stripes within the crust are the boundaries between pieces of crust. The larger orange spots in the center and along the edge of the pool are places where volcanic fumes are bubbling off.

Two spreading zones (the orange stripes, which are about 3 feet wide) in the Mauna Ulu pool of lava are connected by horizontal sliding along a transform fault.

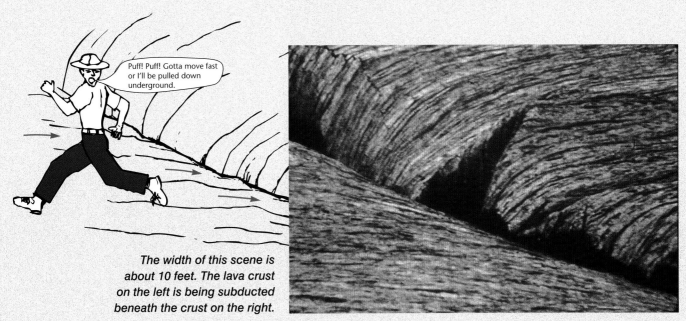

The width of this scene is about 10 feet. The lava crust on the left is being subducted beneath the crust on the right.

The crust of the lava-lake version of plate tectonics didn't include thick masses of light material to imitate Earth's continents. There were no collision zones like the one where India is smashing into Asia. Also, at collision zones both plates often bent and disappeared downward into the lava lake together, rather than one staying at the surface. Nevertheless, the similarities to plate tectonics help people visualize how the much slower big-picture process works.

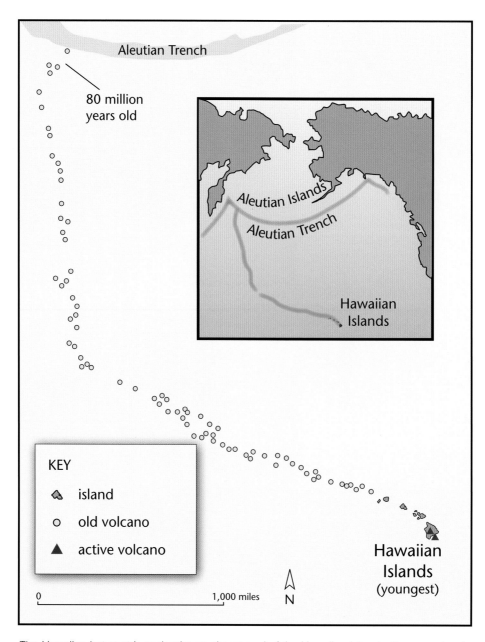

Aleutian Trench

80 million
years old

Aleutian Islands

Aleutian Trench

Hawaiian
Islands

KEY

🔶 island

○ old volcano

▲ active volcano

Hawaiian
Islands
(youngest)

0   1,000 miles

N

The Hawaiian hot spot is under the southeast end of the Hawaiian Islands. Former volcanic islands, now eroded below sea level, mark the path of the Pacific Plate over the hot spot. The direction of the plate's movement changed about 40 million years ago, as shown by the bend in the chain of old volcanoes.

Sunset Crater and other volcanoes that originated in the interior of continental plates are reminders that even though most volcanoes form along plate boundaries, they seem to be able to pop up almost anywhere. Unless a mantle plume is involved, as at Yellowstone, why volcanoes appear within plates is puzzling. The explanation must be related to the heat-driven turbulence in the mantle. If scientists could accurately map the detailed pattern of convection cells and plumes in the mantle, an explanation might emerge. But even the most powerful and sophisticated instruments we have today can create only a primitive map of the mantle's movements.

Sunset Crater (upper left), *near Flagstaff, Arizona, erupted about 1,000 years ago. At that time many Native Americans lived in the area. Their homes were buried by volcanic cinders, but they were able to escape. This volcano is an example of an eruption within the interior of the North American Plate.*

Eruption of Redoubt Volcano, Alaska, on April 21, 1990. A towering column of steam, volcanic fumes, and gritty ash rises thousands of feet, spreading out into the layers of the atmosphere. The eruption at the top of the stratovolcano (the snow-covered peak at lower left) produced hot rock that tumbled downslope in a landslide. At the base of the volcano it flowed into water and triggered steam explosions that produced the ash column.
—PHOTO COURTESY OF J. WARREN, U.S. GEOLOGICAL SURVEY

Why Does Some MAGMA Flow and Some MAGMA Blow?

Some volcanoes are several thousand feet tall, with sides that get steeper toward the top. Others are less than 1,000 feet tall, with sides that are gentler toward the top. Some volcanoes produce lava flows that are many miles long but not even 100 feet thick. Others erupt lava flows that are as thick as they are long. Some volcanoes partly destroy themselves and spew out pyroclastic flows and billowing clouds of ash and pumice, collectively called *tephra*, that cover hundreds of square miles during violent eruptions. Others erupt so gently that observers can safely stand nearby to watch and photograph.

A big reason for such variety in volcano size, shape, and eruptive style is that magma comes in many varieties with different chemical compositions, which control two important properties of the magma: viscosity and volatile content. Viscosity is the resistance of a fluid to flow. A fluid with low viscosity flows much more easily than one with high viscosity, so low-viscosity lava flows long distances in thin layers, whereas high-viscosity lava tends to form thick short flows. Volatiles are vapors (mostly water, carbon dioxide, and sulfur compounds) dissolved in the magma. When pressure on magma is reduced, volatiles escape by boiling off as gases. Volatiles easily rise through and escape from low-viscosity magma, but volatiles trapped in high-viscosity magma can trigger an explosive eruption when they finally break free.

Another factor behind the variety of volcano shapes and eruptive styles is simply the amount of magma available for an eruption. If there isn't much magma, not much of a volcano can be built.

Most magma is created by partially melting mantle rocks. This magma has the chemical composition that geologists call *basalt*. If it steadily rises up from the mantle to the

27

surface and erupts, it quickly cools and solidifies. Magma of basalt composition becomes basalt rock. Because this basalt magma, melted straight from the mantle, is the underlying source for magma of other compositions, many geologists consider it the parent of all other magmas.

Geologists give the names *basalt*, *andesite*, *dacite*, and *rhyolite* to magmas and their corresponding volcanic rocks. These four types are defined by the amount of silica (SiO_2) they contain, which is the way chemists report the amount of the element silicon. If the silica content is about 50 percent, the rock is basalt. Around 58 percent it's andesite. At more or less 65 percent it's dacite. And at about 75 percent it's rhyolite. If you have a volcanic rock and want to be sure what name to give it, you'd need to analyze its silica content.

In nature, the range in magma's silica content from basalt through rhyolite is a continuous gradation, and the boundaries that define the different rock names aren't agreed upon by all geologists. The difference may be just 1 or 2 percent of silica, but sometimes the andesite of Nancy Knows is the dacite of Seymour Says. This good-natured hairsplitting (and stubbornness) is captured in a popular saying among geologists: "If every geologist in the world was laid out end to end, like a bunch of matchsticks, no two would be parallel!" Still, most of them would be almost parallel.

So, how does basalt magma get enriched with silica to become andesite, dacite, or rhyolite? Sometimes magma stops along its way toward the surface. As it sits underground, its chemical composition begins to change. If the stop is brief, the change may be minor, perhaps producing a slightly different variety of basalt. With more time, though, magma very different from basalt can be created.

Whether the change is small or big, it happens in three ways. The most common way is when basalt magma cools enough for mineral crystals to start growing. The first crystals that form, olivine and pyroxene, are rich in iron, magnesium, and calcium, poor in silica, and don't contain volatiles. These minerals are denser than the remaining magma so they can sink. As that remaining magma continues its upward journey, it's now poorer in iron, magnesium, and calcium and richer in silica and volatiles than when the journey began.

The second way basalt magma becomes enriched with silica is when it melts nearby rock in the crust, which is almost always richer in silica than basalt magma. The mixture of basalt magma and melted crust rock contains more silica than the original magma did.

The third way is when rising basalt magma encounters another batch of magma already in the crust and the two mix. Once again, the most likely outcome is a mixture high in silica relative to pure basalt magma because the magma already in the crust has probably become enriched with silica by the first two processes.

There's plenty of silicon and oxygen in all magmas—rhyolite, dacite, andesite, and basalt. Groups of silicon and oxygen atoms cluster into a pyramid structure in which the four corners are silicon, surrounding a single, smaller oxygen atom. Neighboring

Type of Volcanic Rock	Melting Temperature	Silica Content (SiO_2)	Magma Characteristics
RHYOLITE	1,400°F	68-77%	high gas, explosive, thick, sticky
DACITE		63-68%	
ANDESITE		52-63%	
BASALT	2,200°F	48-52%	low gas, less explosive, thin, runny

Melting temperatures, silica content, and magma characteristics of different types of volcanic rock.

pyramids bond strongly to each other, and magma viscosity is a direct function of this pyramid-to-pyramid bonding. So magma with the most silica (rhyolite) has the greatest viscosity because it has more of those tightly bonded pyramids, while magma with the least silica (basalt) has the lowest viscosity. For comparison, think about the fluidity (viscosity) of water versus that of honey. In the world of magma, basalt is the water version and rhyolite is the honey version—sort of. Water is about five thousand times more fluid than honey, but basalt magma is about ten million times more fluid than rhyolite.

As described above, when basalt magma changes into andesite, dacite, or rhyolite magma, the gassiness (volatile content) of the new magma increases. This is important to keep in mind, because more volatiles and higher viscosity create a lot more potential for violent eruptions.

As basalt magma rises to the surface and the pressure decreases, the dissolved gases can bubble off fairly easily because of the low viscosity of the magma. So basalt eruptions usually aren't very violent. In stark contrast, the abundant volatiles in rhyolite magma have a very difficult time moving through and escaping from the thick, viscous magma. When these bubbles finally do break free, they tend to produce powerful explosive eruptions of broken rock. Eruptions of andesite and dacite magmas fall somewhere between the extremes of rhyolite and basalt.

A kitchen-table experiment can help illustrate the difference in how gases move through liquids with different viscosities. Fill a glass with water, to represent basalt magma, and another with honey, to represent rhyolite magma. Insert a straw deeply into each, blow gently, and observe how bubbles rise through the liquid and break to the surface—and be prepared to clean up a mess!

THE FAMILY OF VOLCANOES

Volcanoes have life spans ranging from a few years to a million years or more. Some begin life as one type of volcano and mature into another, and a variety of volcano types often grow atop one another. The following sections discuss specific types of volcanoes, but keep in mind that as the magma supply and chemistry change, the volcanoe type at the surface also may change.

CINDER CONES

Basalt cinder cones are the most common kind of volcano worldwide. They are also some of the smallest volcanoes. A typical eruption goes through two stages. The first is called the *fountaining stage*. When the basalt magma first breaks out at the surface, the dissolved gases bubble off vigorously enough to carry blobs of magma into the air with them. The blobs may rise up 2,000 feet or more. During their flight through the air, the blobs cool to solid pieces called *cinders* (also called *scoria*), which are typically no bigger than a softball. These spongelike rocks contain holes, called *vesicles*, where gas bubbles got trapped inside. As the cinders fall back to Earth, they form layers that pile up into a cone-shaped hill. The very top, where magma spewed out, usually ends up as a small crater. Once most of the gassy magma has erupted, fountaining stops.

During the second stage, gas-poor basalt magma continues to erupt. It burrows out beneath the base of the cinder cone because it doesn't contain as many dissolved gases, so it's denser than the spongelike cinders. As a result, the cinder cone can literally float atop the denser lava. Sometimes big chunks of the cone float away with the lava as it oozes out of the base and moves downhill. Because of its relatively low viscosity, a basalt lava flow may travel many miles from its cinder cone before it cools enough to become solid rock.

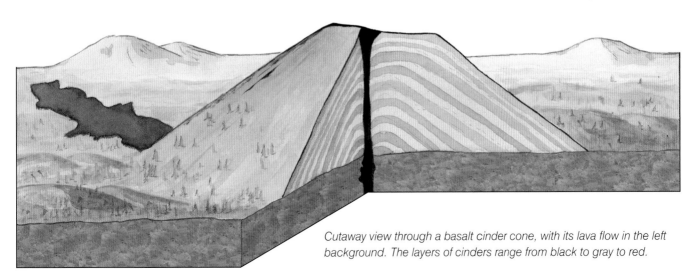

Cutaway view through a basalt cinder cone, with its lava flow in the left background. The layers of cinders range from black to gray to red.

SP Crater in the San Francisco Volcanic Field near Flagstaff, Arizona, is an example of a basalt cinder cone and lava flow. The cone is about 900 feet tall. The flow, extending from the cone to the upper right of this photo, is 4 miles long and about 100 feet thick. Note that two fingers of lava on the left spilled into a preexisting valley. The cinder cone of the SP Crater erupted several thousand years ago.

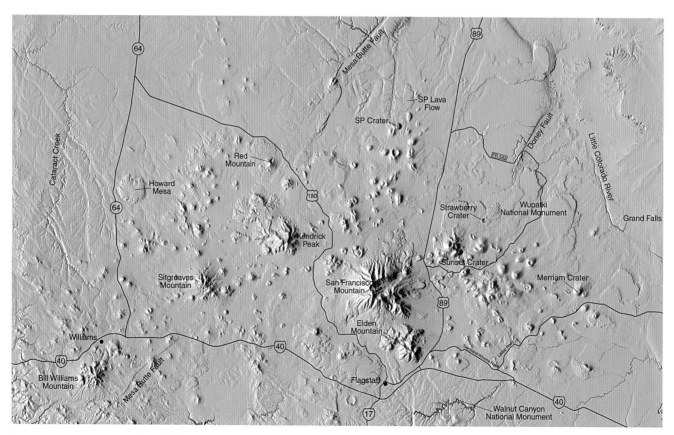

The San Francisco Volcanic Field in northern Arizona contains about six hundred basalt cinder cones. All of the hills in this shaded relief image are cinder cones except the half-dozen larger hills, where lava from many eruptions piled up. The oldest cinder cones in the image are 6 million years old, and the youngest (Sunset Crater) is only about 1,000 years old. The distance from left to right is 50 miles.

Cinder cone volcanoes often occur in clusters, called *volcanic fields*. A field typically covers tens or hundreds of square miles. The life span of an individual cinder cone is likely to be just a few years or less, but the development of an entire field may last several million years. In 1943, a basalt cinder cone eruption began in a cornfield in Mexico. Nine years later, the eruption stopped. The cone, named Paricutín, had grown to be nearly 1,400 feet tall, and its lava flow extended about 4 miles to the north.

CORN ROCK

When the basalt cinder cone at Sunset Crater erupted about 1,000 years ago near present-day Flagstaff, Arizona, many nearby homes of Native Americans were destroyed. Perhaps in attempts to placate the volcano spirit, they offered corn—their most important food crop—to the erupting volcano. Lava that splashed down on the ears of corn quickly chilled, creating perfect casts, right down to the outlines of individual kernels. These casts are called *corn rock*. The corn either burned, or soon rotted away after the molten lava chilled and solidified around it. Some corn rocks were used in the construction of Native American homes in nearby villages shortly after the eruption.

A corn rock was formed when lava solidified around an ear of corn Native Americans offered to an erupting volcano in northern Arizona. Notice the perfect cast of the ear of corn and its individual kernels.

As part of a team of geologists and archaeologists who study corn rocks, I visited Kilauea Volcano to create corn rocks similar to those found at Sunset Crater in Arizona. In the background, lava meets waves of the Pacific Ocean.

Mauna Loa Volcano in Hawaii illustrates the gentle slopes and shield shape of a basalt shield volcano. The flanks of the volcano extend many miles to the right and left. —PHOTO COURTESY OF BEN GADDIS, U.S. GEOLOGICAL SURVEY

SHIELD VOLCANOES

When many eruptions of basalt magma occur at one place, over a long period of time, the lava flows build up into a tall, wide, layered stack called a *shield volcano*. Because of the magma's low viscosity, each flow extends out a great distance from the spot where the magma emerged onto the surface. But because cooling to solid rock begins as soon as the magma emerges, more lava builds up near the center of the volcano than at a great distance. The final shape of the mountain is like an ancient warrior's bowed shield laid on the ground, hump-side up.

Many of the world's classic shield volcanoes are in Hawaii. An excellent example is Mauna Loa, which tops out at nearly 14,000 feet above sea level. At sea level, the mountain is about 75 miles wide from coast to coast. On the seafloor, about 15,000 feet below sea level, it's about 150 miles wide. The base of the volcano's lava flows actually lies about 40,000 feet below sea level because the weight of the thickest part of this gigantic mountain has pushed down the seafloor on which it sits.

Geologists estimate that Mauna Loa first erupted about 1 million years ago but didn't emerge above sea level until about 400,000 years ago. And the mountain is still growing! The most recent eruption, as of the time this book was published, was in 1984.

As they grow, large shield volcanoes develop a reservoir of magma within the shield. It's a kind of a storage container from which magma erupts when the tank is filled beyond its capacity by more magma rising from the mantle. Large shield volcanoes also develop two or three widely spaced steep cracks, called *rift zones*, that radiate out from the top like the spokes of a bicycle wheel. Eruptions occur along these rifts, as well as at the top. If enough magma quickly leaves the reservoir through a rift zone, the top of the shield sinks to form a summit depression called a *caldera*.

Shield volcanoes much smaller than those in Hawaii can form when the volume of magma from the source in the mantle is much smaller—and isn't gassy enough to make a cinder cone instead. Sometimes small shield volcanoes occur within fields of basalt cinder cones.

FLOOD BASALTS

Several times during Earth's long history, massive outpourings of basalt magma have buried huge areas with thick piles of lava flows. The magma gushed out rapidly, flooding these areas with a sheet of lava that solidified into a horizontal layer. The outpouring was repeated many times, so the landscape has stacked lava flows but no central volcano.

In areas of flood basalt, magma didn't emerge onto the surface in one place and pile up. Instead, it emerged from cracks that can be many miles long. In regions with flood basalts, geologists have found many parallel steep cracks filled with solid basalt, called *dikes*, that represent the passageways through which the magma flowed onto the surface. Magma apparently gushed out so fast that it didn't have time to cool enough to build a volcanic mountain at the surface over the crack. But when the eruption stopped, any magma remaining underground in the crack cooled and solidified, becoming a dike.

Geologists think that flood basalts occur over mantle plumes that produce an especially large volume of magma in a short period of time. The magma accumulates in or below the crust repeatedly in vast volumes that erupt in a rapid sequence of floods onto the surface.

Some flood basalt areas are on ocean floors and difficult to study under all that water. About a dozen flood basalt areas are on continents. These range in area from 77,000 to 580,000 square miles (more than twice the size of Texas) and in thickness from 6,500 to 40,000 feet. Many of these accumulated in less than 1 million years.

The Deccan flood basalt of India erupted around the time that dinosaurs became extinct. Some geologists think that the gases that bubbled off during the eruption changed Earth's atmosphere enough to cause this extinction, and also to wipe out lots of other plant and animal life. However, a powerful meteorite impact at Chicxulub in Mexico coincided with these extinctions. That impact also might have changed Earth's atmosphere and climate enough to wipe out many groups of plants and animals. Maybe the massive basalt eruption and meteor impact combined for a deadly one-two punch.

The oldest known flood basalt erupted about 4 billion years ago, not long after planet Earth formed. The youngest, the Columbia Plateau basalt, formed between about 17 and 16 million years ago. It covers a third of Washington State and parts of Oregon and Idaho.

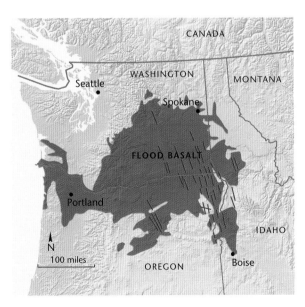

Distribution of the Columbia Plateau flood basalt (brown) in Washington, Oregon, and Idaho. Red lines represent traces of cracks through which the basalt erupted. Some of the lava flowed all the way to the Pacific Ocean.

This dike, a vertical sheet of basalt, cuts across horizontal beds of sedimentary rock. Dikes like this mark the passageway through which magma rose from its source in the mantle toward a site of eruption at Earth's surface. When the eruption stops, magma left in the passageway solidifies into rock. —PHOTO COURTESY OF PAUL DELANEY, U.S. GEOLOGICAL SURVEY

A 3,000-foot thickness of Columbia Plateau flood basalt in northeastern Oregon contains many individual flows. Each horizontal rib is a resistant layer within a single flow. —PHOTO COURTESY OF DON SWANSON, U.S. GEOLOGICAL SURVEY

Snow-capped Mount Fuji, a stratovolcano in Japan, as seen across Lake Ashi. —PHOTO COURTESY OF LEE SIEBERT, SMITHSONIAN INSTITUTION

STRATOVOLCANOES

When asked to draw a picture of a volcano, most people sketch the shape of a strato-volcano, also called a *stratocone* or *composite volcano*. Perhaps the most widely known is Japan's Mount Fuji, with its classic stratovolcano shape. Mount Hood in Oregon is one of the best-known stratovolcanoes in the United States. Stratovolcanoes range in height from a few thousand feet to more than 10,000 feet.

The slopes of stratovolcanoes usually steepen toward the top. Most stratovolca-noes are located above subduction zones, where one tectonic plate is sliding beneath another. In these settings, individual volcanoes are spaced many miles apart. They form chains that are parallel to the ocean-floor trench where one tectonic plate is colliding with and sliding beneath a neighboring plate. In oceanic settings like the western Pacific Ocean and the Aleutian Islands of Alaska, the volcanoes are arranged in long chains that gently arc with the curvature of the Earth.

A stratovolcano is built up by many eruptions over a period that can last 1 million years or longer. It continues to grow as long as the underlying subduction zone cre-ates magma. Most of the erupted magma is andesite, although stratovolcanoes com-monly erupt some basalt, dacite, and rhyolite magmas, too.

Because andesite magma is more viscous than basalt, an andesite lava flows doesn't travel as far from its vent before it solidifies to hard rock. A flow that starts at the top may not even get to the base of the volcano. Or it may reach the base but not go much farther. Because andesite magma usually contains more dissolved gases than basalt does, it tends to erupt violently more often. Many andesite eruptions produce abundant cinders and other broken pieces of volcanic rock, which collectively are called *tephra* in all volcanic eruptions. Tephra includes small particles of ash. Over many years, a stratovolcano becomes a steep-sided mountain composed of alternating layers of solid lava flows and loose tephra. The name *composite volcano* emphasizes this interlayering of lava and tephra.

The steep slopes of stratovolcanoes are so unstable that material often breaks free and slumps downhill as landslides. Some of these landslides are caused solely by the pull of gravity, as multiple eruptions build a slope to increasingly steep angles. Earthquake shaking can trigger landslides, too, and earthquakes are common in subduction zones. Heavy rainfall is another cause of landslides.

Antarctica is home to one of Earth's most fascinating stratovolcanoes, Mount Erebus. Its summit crater contains a restless lava lake that has 4-inch-long crystals of the mineral feldspar floating around in it—the only lava lake with such crystals.

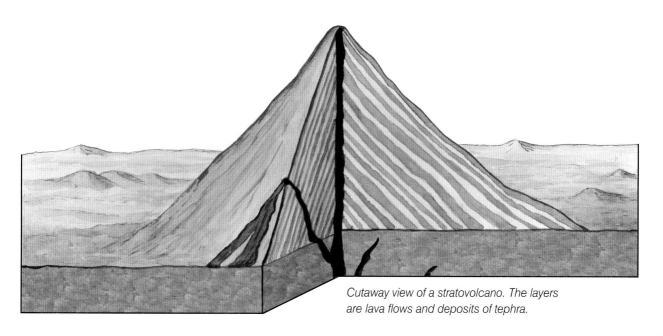

Cutaway view of a stratovolcano. The layers are lava flows and deposits of tephra.

Although most stratovolcano eruptions begin at the top of the mountain, magma can also push out to the side before reaching the top. This can create a blisterlike bump on the flank of the mountain. That magma-caused bump can burst into a violent eruption if magma breaks free to the surface, especially dacite or rhyolite magma.

Mount St. Helens, near Vancouver, Washington, is a stratovolcano. Leading up to the spectacular eruption of May 18, 1980, magma rising inside the mountain started to push out toward the north before reaching the top. During a period of a few weeks, this created a large blisterlike bulge on the side of the volcano. Eventually the bulge became unstable and fell away in a huge landslide, exposing the cause of the bulge: new dacite magma. It erupted violently as its volatiles became suddenly free to escape. The entire north side and core of Mount St. Helens slipped and was blasted

Mount St. Helens as seen from the north on May 17, 1980. A large bulge had grown on this side of the volcano (near the left end of the lower cloud formation) because of magma pushing out from within the mountain. —PHOTO COURTESY OF KEITH RONNHOLM

The eruption of Mount St. Helens begins on May 18, 1980, at about 8:30 a.m. Pacific Daylight Time.
—PHOTO COURTESY OF KEITH RONNHOLM

Several seconds later, Mount St. Helens is almost completely hidden by the growing cloud of tephra. —PHOTO COURTESY OF KEITH RONNHOLM

Aerial view of Mount St. Helens in 1983. Fumes rise from a dacite lava dome growing in the large crater that formed on May 18, 1980.

away. When the air cleared, a gigantic new amphitheatre-shaped crater was revealed. In the thirty years since the 1980 eruption, subsequent eruptions have partly filled the blasted-out crater. Perhaps the volcano will heal itself back into the shape of a perfectly formed stratovolcano in the not-too-distant geologic future.

LAVA DOMES

As the name says, a lava dome volcano is a roughly dome-shaped mountain—a bit like half a sphere with a lumpy surface. Most lava domes are less than 1 cubic mile in volume and no more than 2,000 feet tall. They have very steep sides because they're made of viscous dacite and rhyolite magmas. High viscosity limits how far lava can flow, usually resulting in a pile-up of lava over the vent. Some domes produce tall, pointed spines at the top as they grow, but these spines usually become unstable and collapse. Other domes have rather flat or even slightly sunken tops.

Because dacite and rhyolite are the most volatile-rich of the magmas, dome-forming eruptions begin with an explosive phase as the magma's dissolved gases burst free into the atmosphere. This phase creates deposits of coarse tephra in a ring around the vent, and often a blanket of smaller particles that drapes the downwind landscape. Once the explosive phase is over, the remaining magma, now depleted of volatiles but still very viscous, oozes out and builds a steep-sided mountain. Dome building can result in two different types of internal structure: endogenous or exogenous.

An endogenous dome grows from within (in Greek, *endo* means "inside"), somewhat like an inflating balloon. As magma emerges from the vent, the dome expands above it. Unlike a balloon, though, the outer skin of the dome isn't elastic, so it can't stretch. Instead, the outer part quickly chills to form solid rock that breaks into pieces as the liquid magma core continues pushing upward and outward. The insulation provided by the outer broken layer helps keep the inside molten.

An 80,000-year-old, 1,800-foot-wide endogenous rhyolite lava dome at Coso, California. Note the lumpy, sunken top of the dome. The smooth arc-shaped ground to the left of the dome is a deposit of tephra produced in the initial explosive phase of eruption. A younger black basalt lava flow partly surrounds the dome.

At the end of the eruption, the volcano is a dome-shaped mountain wrapped in the cover of broken rock, which is called *carapace breccia*. Beneath that breccia, the dome is solid rock. The top of an endogenous dome may be flat or a shallow closed crater, probably because some of the magma core sinks back underground through the vent at the end of eruption.

Novarupta, an endogenous rhyolite lava dome, formed in less than four years after an initial explosive phase in 1912 produced the tephra that formed the Valley of Ten Thousand Smokes in Alaska.
—PHOTO COURTESY OF WES HILDRETH, U.S. GEOLOGICAL SURVEY

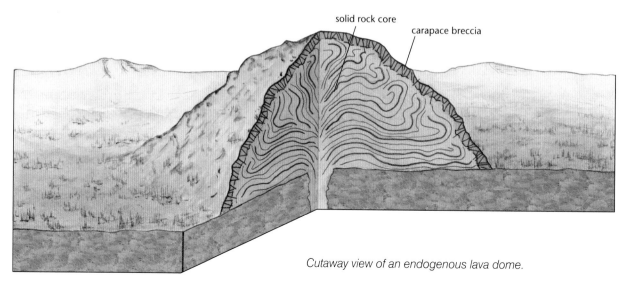

solid rock core

carapace breccia

Cutaway view of an endogenous lava dome.

An exogenous dome starts to grow like its endogenous counterpart but eventually adds layers of new material to the outside of the volcano (Greek *exo* means "outside"). When this happens, magma breaks through the early carapace breccia, covers it with solid lava, and produces its own carapace breccia. This kind of breakout can happen several times. At the end of the eruption, the outside of the dome is wrapped in a cover of carapace breccia, like its endogenous cousin. But the inside also includes layers of breccia as well as solid lava.

Elden Mountain at Flagstaff, Arizona, is a 2,000-foot-tall dacite lava dome. The overlapping lobes and fingers of the mountainside are evidence of the volcano's exogenous origin. Because the eruption happened about 500,000 years ago, the outside breccia has been eroded away.

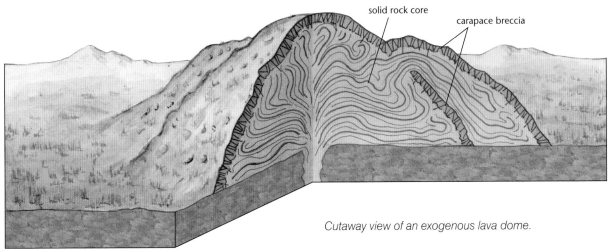

Cutaway view of an exogenous lava dome.

The reason that some lava domes become exogenous may relate to how long an eruption lasts. If eruption occurs in a single uninterrupted episode of magma extrusion, the core of the growing dome is likely to stay liquid beneath the insulating blanket of carapace breccia. However, if growth happens in brief spurts over a long period of time, the core could cool enough to solidify before the next pulse of eruption occurs. That new magma would break its way through the solid core and erupt as a new layer over the previously formed carapace breccia.

The growth of three exogenous lava domes has been closely observed. The continuing eruption at Santiaguito in Guatemala began in 1922 and that at Soufrière Hills Volcano, at Montserrat in the Caribbean, began in 1995. The post-1980 dome at Mount St. Helens is presently dormant. All three domes, which formed over several decades, have gone through alternating periods of growth and dormancy.

By contrast, the endogenous dome Novarupta in Alaska formed in less than four years—and maybe much less. No one visited the eruption site until four years after the 1912 eruption of tephra that formed the Valley of Ten Thousand Smokes. The growth of the Novarupta dome was the final phase of that eruption. Prehistoric domes like those of the Coso Volcanic Field in California appear to be as structurally simple as that of Novarupta and so may have formed quickly enough to be endogenous.

Some eruptions that begin as lava domes evolve into lava flows. The shape and slope of the landscape is critical in whether this happens. When viscous dacite and rhyolite magmas erupt onto a flat surface, a steep-sided circular dome will probably result. But if magma erupts onto a sloping surface, even highly viscous lava will flow downhill, resulting in a fingerlike shape, called a *coulee*, a French word for flow. For erupting magma of any viscosity, the steeper the landscape, the farther it can flow before cooling changes hot molten lava to solid rock.

VIOLENT CALDERA-FORMING PYROCLASTIC ERUPTIONS

It may seem strange, but the sites of some of the world's largest and most violent volcanic eruptions are not obvious, tall, majestic mountains. In fact, at a few miles away from the volcano's center, viewers may not realize that they're standing on the broad shoulder of one of these humongous creatures. Upslope and out of sight, the main volcanic landscape feature is a hole in the ground, called a *caldera*, rather than an imposing mountain that rises steeply thousands of feet above its surroundings. At a distance of a few miles, the viewer would probably be standing on a layer of tephra erupted from the caldera.

The volume of magma that erupts to build a stratovolcano, a cinder cone, or a lava dome is generally less than a cubic mile or two. In each case, the new volcano is an obvious hill or mountain. In stark contrast, the volume of magma involved in caldera-forming eruptions is hundreds of cubic miles, or even more than 1,000 cubic

Oregon's Crater Lake fills a caldera. The white areas are snow. The caldera-forming eruption occurred about 7,700 years ago. The caldera is 6 miles wide, and the lake within it is as much as 1,932 feet deep. Wizard Island, on the near side of the lake, is a small andesite stratovolcano that grew up from the caldera floor a few hundred years after the caldera formed. —PHOTO COURTESY OF MIKE DOUKAS, U.S. GEOLOGICAL SURVEY

miles. The erupted material is mostly spread in a blanketlike layer of tephra around and downwind of the caldera.

Calderas form when a large reservoir of volatile-rich dacite or rhyolite magma in the crust reaches conditions where the overlying lid of rocks can no longer hold in the magma. An enormous eruption then occurs. When so much magma erupts quickly, the ground sinks into the space where magma had been stored, and that sinkhole is the caldera.

A stream has eroded into this ash-flow tuff, composed of tephra ejected from Crater Lake Caldera (just out of view upslope in the background). The change in color reflects chemical change in magma from the material that erupted first (the light color at the base) to the material that erupted later (the gray layer on top).
—PHOTO COURTESY OF CHARLES BACON, U.S. GEOLOGICAL SURVEY

How long does a caldera-forming eruption last? No caldera-forming eruption of silica-rich magma has ever been observed, but geologists have gathered strong evidence that the eruption that formed Long Valley Caldera in California, 760,000 years ago, lasted about six days. During that busy week, 145 cubic miles of magma were erupted. For planet Earth, whose life spans 4.55 billion years, six days is less than a snap of the fingers is to a human life.

As volatiles escape from the highly viscous magma, they drag along blobs of molten rock that quickly solidify and break into fragments of rock and minerals as gas bubbles burst free. (Bubbles that stay trapped inside create a frothy rock called *pumice*.) The smallest fragments rise thousands of feet into the air, where wind may carry them many miles away. The heavier pieces fall back to the land surface first, and the lighter

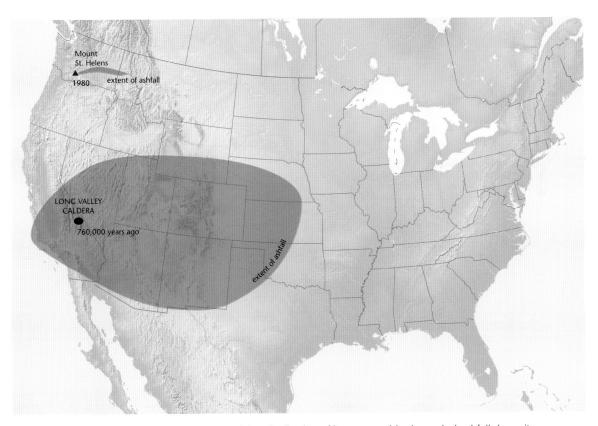

California's Long Valley Caldera and the distribution of its measurable downwind ashfall deposit. Notice how much smaller the comparable deposit is for Mount St. Helens.

pieces fall later. Together, they form a tongue-shaped deposit that covers the down-wind landscape.

The much larger and heavier tephra falls back to the land surface inside and just outside the subsiding caldera. Outside, it flows away as hot mixtures of rock and mineral fragments suspended in the gases that escape from the magma. Some air from the atmosphere gets mixed in too, and helps cushion the ride of the fragments. After a surface-hugging flow comes to rest and solidifies into rock, it's called *ash-flow tuff*.

The cliffs of the top third of this outcrop are 1.3-million-year-old ash-flow tuffs. Their eruption created New Mexico's Valles Caldera, which lies several miles to the west. The slope with trees is 1.6-million-year-old ash-flow tuff. Its eruption created a caldera now buried beneath Valles Caldera. The white deposit is also 1.6 million years old and is the material that erupted first during the older caldera-forming event. Below, the person is standing on a black basalt lava flow that's 2.4 million years old.
—PHOTO COURTESY OF CATHY GOFF

Tephra that falls back into the caldera partly fills what would otherwise be a much deeper hole. Calderas range from several to many miles wide and from hundreds to a few thousand feet deep. Most have a circular or oval outline, depending on the shape of the preeruption magma reservoir and the pattern of cracks in the crust that the magma pushed through when it erupted.

Some shallow calderas seem to have just sagged down into the space vacated by the magma reservoir, rather than breaking free and sinking like a piston of rock. The floors of other calderas sink like the hinged flap of a trapdoor, rather than breaking completely free and dropping down the same amount all the way around. Whatever their shape, and regardless of how the overlying ground collapsed, many calderas are so large that they're most readily recognized in views from high above, rather than on the ground.

It takes a continuous supply of heat energy over a long period of time to build up a big enough reservoir of dacite or rhyolite magma in the crust to produce a caldera-forming eruption. The heat comes from basalt magma rising up from the mantle. As the magma cools and changes chemically, and also partially melts the surrounding crust, it becomes enriched in silica, creating dacite and rhyolite magmas. The time needed to create a large enough reservoir of silica-rich magma to become a caldera volcano ranges up to a few million years.

During the buildup time, some of the basalt magma erupts as cinder cones. In addition, some of the newly created silica-enriched magma collecting in the crust erupts to form lava domes and coulees. But these cinder cones, domes, and coulees are just piddling small-volume leaks from the huge amount of magma rising from the mantle, evolving in the crust, and changing composition there beneath the future caldera site. A stratovolcano might even grow during the time leading up to the eruption of a caldera volcano.

From about 4 million years ago to a bit less than 1 million years ago, eruptions that created basalt cinder cones and dacite and rhyolite lava domes occurred in the area that later became Long Valley Caldera in California. In Oregon, many small eruptions, starting about 1 million years ago, eventually built Mount Mazama, a stratovolcano, over the place where a violent eruption created Crater Lake Caldera 7,700 years ago. The volume of magma erupted at Crater Lake Caldera was only 15 cubic miles, compared to 145 cubic miles for Long Valley. That's probably because the lead-up period was so much shorter at Crater Lake. The more time there is for basalt magma to rise up from the mantle and create silica-enriched magma, the greater the volume of magma that can eventually erupt to form a caldera.

Shortly after a caldera forms, eruptions of rhyolite and dacite lava domes and basalt cinder cones may occur on the caldera's floor and just outside the caldera. Once the volatile-rich magma has erupted violently, any magma remaining in the reservoir can leak out. As this leftover magma pushes up to erupt, it usually bows up the middle part of the floor of the caldera into a blisterlike shape.

Snow-covered Aniakchak Caldera in Alaska formed 3,500 years ago when about 12 cubic miles of magma erupted. The caldera is 6 miles wide and 3,000 feet deep. At the far side, a canyon cuts across the caldera wall. Were it not for that canyon this caldera would hold a lake and look a lot like Crater Lake in Oregon, right down to the new volcano that has grown since the caldera formed, which would be much like Wizard Island.
—PHOTO COURTESY OF M. WILLIAMS, NATIONAL PARK SERVICE

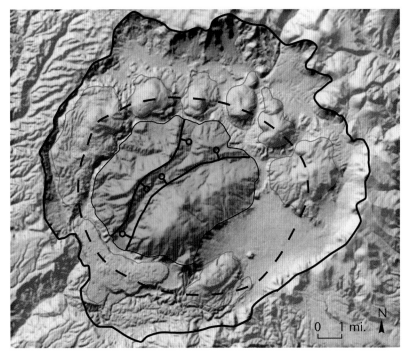

——————— Present-day topographic rim of the caldera

– – – Surface trace of the fault along which the caldera collapsed

⟍ᵔ⟍ᵔ Faults

☐ Headwalls of landslides from the originally steep
caldera walls and sediment on the caldera floor

☐ Postcaldera rhyolite domes and flows

☐ Dome pushed up by magma remaining in reservoir
after eruption

☐ Precaldera rocks

*New Mexico's Valles Caldera originally contained a lake. When the lake over-
flowed the caldera wall, it eroded a valley (bottom left) that drained the lake. If
basalt magma continues to rise from the mantle for a long time after a caldera
forms, a second caldera eruption can occur in the same area. Valles Caldera has
been through two cycles of caldera eruption, one 1.6 million years ago, and the
other 1.3 million years ago. The younger caldera formed right on top of and has
completely buried the older one. All features shown here are part of the younger
caldera.* —SHADED RELIEF COURTESY OF FRASER GOFF

SUPERVOLCANOES

On February 3, 2000, the British Broadcasting Corporation aired a program called "Supervolcanoes," about extremely large caldera-forming eruptions, in the popular television series *Horizons*. Research scientists have adopted this concept and are working toward a strict definition of the term *supervolcano*. The Volcanic Explosivity Index (VEI) comes in handy here. On this scale, which runs from 0 to 8 or higher, an eruption classified as VEI 8 spews out more than 240 cubic miles of magma and erupts ash and fumes more than 16 miles into the atmosphere. Some say that a good definition of a supervolcano is any eruption with a VEI of at least 8. Throughout the known geologic record, no eruption higher than VEI 8 has yet been identified.

The main problem in establishing a single agreed-upon definition is that there have been no supervolcano eruptions during recorded human history. The two most recent happened in New Zealand with Lake Taupo's Oruanui eruption 26,500 years ago and in Sumatra with the Toba Volcano eruption 74,000 years ago. No volcanologists were around to measure the height of the eruption column, but the volume of erupted magma, calculated from the volume of tephra deposits, exceeds 240 cubic miles in each case. Because of erosion, it's difficult to determine the volume of magma erupted during even older caldera-forming events, but several are definitely more than 240 cubic miles, including two of Yellowstone's three caldera-forming eruptions.

There's some evidence that the eruption of Toba 74,000 years ago changed Earth's climate so much for so long that prehistoric human populations were driven almost to extinction. So it's reasonable to suppose that a future supervolcano eruption would be equally devastating to humankind. And because Earth's human population is so much greater now, the number of deaths could be huge.

The good news is that supervolcano eruptions are rare. So far, only about fifty have been identified throughout Earth's 4.55-billion-year life span. The 2000 episode of *Horizons* claimed, "Scientists know that another one is due—they just don't know when or where" and hinted that Yellowstone may be due, given its history of three supervolcano eruptions at a roughly 800,000- to 660,000-year interval. On the other hand, could it be that Earth has cooled enough during its long life that its internal heat energy isn't sufficient to power more supervolcano eruptions? I personally doubt that, but one can hope!

The Yellowstone Caldera, which is the heart of Yellowstone National Park, is the youngest of three overlapping calderas that are 2.1 million years old, 1.3 million years old, and 640,000 years old. The time between those eruptions is 800,000 and 660,000 years. Because the youngest caldera is now about 640,000 years old, scientists watch the behavior of the Yellowstone area very closely for hints that another caldera-forming eruption might happen there. Most agree that more eruptions will happen. The big questions are when the next eruption will happen, and whether it will produce a cinder cone, a lava dome, or yet another caldera. Many small lava dome eruptions have already occurred within the youngest Yellowstone caldera.

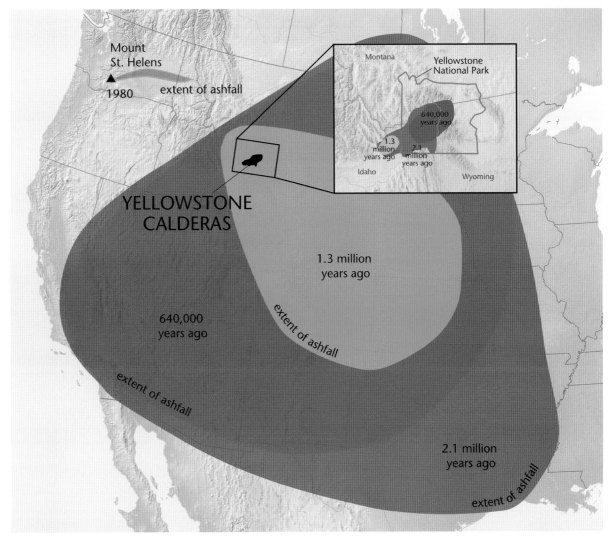

The three Yellowstone calderas and the distribution of their measurable ashfall deposits.

When lava entered the Pacific Ocean along the south coast of Kilauea Volcano, Hawaii, on the night of July 16, 2008, the 2,000-degree-Fahrenheit heat of this molten rock boiled seawater to steam. Bursts of steam carried clots of the molten rock as high as 600 feet in a fiery display watched by the awestruck observers in the lower left foreground of the picture. —PHOTO COURTESY OF MICHAEL POLAND, U.S. GEOLOGICAL SURVEY

What Happens When
MOLTEN ROCK Meets Water?

As you've learned, water and other volatile substances dissolved in magma are the main reason that some eruptions are violent. The greater the amount of dissolved volatiles and the more viscous the magma, the greater the potential for a really explosive eruption as those volatiles burst free just below and at the vent during an eruption.

When rising magma encounters groundwater or when lava encounters the water of an ocean, lake, or stream, it makes for an even more exciting eruption. In addition to releasing its own volatiles (including water vapor), hot molten rock quickly boils groundwater or surface water, producing steam. That steam can either hiss away without much damage to the surroundings or explode in giant, superheated bubbles. It all depends on how much magma or lava there is compared to water, and on how quickly the molten rock's heat is transferred to the water. The greatest potential for a violent effect is when about equal weights of molten rock and water mix quickly. Because of its low viscosity, molten basalt mixes with water most easily.

WHEN MAGMA MEETS GROUNDWATER

When basalt magma mixes with groundwater, bursts of steam blast out blobs of magma and pieces of preexisting rocks, forming a crater at the volcano vent. Cinders and other rocky debris fall back to Earth around and downwind of the vent. With each new blast of steam, the crater gets deeper and wider, and it continues to grow in this way until the magma and water stop mixing. If the supply of available water runs out before the magma does, the eruption can build a cinder cone volcano at the bottom of the crater.

If the crater bottom is below the water table (the top surface of the groundwater), water seeps into the crater to form a lake. For this reason, this type of volcano is called a *maar*, a German word meaning "lake." There are lots of maars in the Eifel region in Germany, the place where it was first recognized that maar volcanoes are formed by powerful steam explosions. Almost all maars are formed by low-viscosity basalt magma, although there's at least one example of a rhyolite maar in Mexico.

Not all maar volcanoes have a crater lake today. For example, about 32,000 years ago eruptions in northern Mexico created several maar volcanoes. But since then, the climate in that area has become arid, and surface water and shallow groundwater have disappeared. Lakebeds and shoreline deposits near the bottom of these craters are all that remain of the lakes that once existed. In the Eifel region of Germany, groundwater is still close enough to the surface to fill the craters with lakes.

Crater Elegante, a maar volcano of the Pinacate Volcanic Field in Sonora, Mexico, is 1 mile wide and 800 feet deep. The eruption occurred about 30,000 years ago. The light-colored deposits around the rim of the crater are products of the eruption. Below them, the darker reddish deposits are the older rocks blasted out by the eruption's steam explosions. The reddish hump along the right side of the crater wall is the remains of a basalt cinder cone volcano that predates the maar eruption. —PHOTO COURTESY OF JIM GUTMANN

Ukinrek maar volcano, Alaska, erupting on April 6, 1977, when basalt magma encountered groundwater and steam blasted out a crater.
—PHOTO COURTESY OF RICHARD RUSSELL, ALASKA DEPARTMENT OF FISH AND GAME

Ukinrek maar volcano in 1993. The dark-colored layered rocks in the crater wall and on the surrounding landscape are basalt products of the eruption. The light-colored rocks below are the preexisting rocks in which the crater was blasted out. The final phase of the eruption produced a small basalt cinder cone that is now under water. The crater is 1,000 feet wide.
—PHOTO COURTESY OF DAVID LESCINSKY

WHEN LAVA MEETS SURFACE WATER

When a small volume of lava slowly spills into a body of water, water overwhelms the lava, chilling it so quickly that the flow solidifies to volcanic glass, which immediately cracks and breaks into pieces. A glass bottle or cup will do the same thing if heated and then quickly dunked into cold water. Basalt lava frequently flows into the Pacific Ocean along the seashores of Hawaii. Like pieces of a recently broken glass bottle, the newly shattered lava has sharp edges that can cut bare feet. Over time, the surf erodes the sharp edges and produces the smooth, rounded sand grains of Hawaii's famous black sand beaches.

Sometimes a narrow basalt lava flow triggers nearly continuous steam explosions where it enters the ocean. If this action continues long enough, a cone-shaped pile of cinders builds up. The cone looks just like cinder cones that form during eruptions on dry land, but it doesn't have the direct connection to magma rising from the mantle via a crack underneath.

When a large amount of lava flows into the ocean fast enough, some of it remains molten as it advances into the water, where a thin skin solidifies over its surface,

This growing stack of pillow lava was photographed by a remote-controlled submersible (called Jason) during the eruption of West Mata Volcano in May of 2009, at a depth of 4,000 feet. Note the orange molten rock peeking through cracks in the skin of the expanding pillows. Each pillow is about 3 feet long. The volcano is 120 miles southwest of Samoa in the southwest Pacific Ocean. —PHOTO COURTESY OF KEN RUBIN, UNIVERSITY OF HAWAII

This outcrop in Oman, a country at the southeast corner of the Arabian Peninsula, provides a cross-sectional view through a stack of pillow lava. Each pillow is 1 to 2 feet across and a bit longer than wide. These rocks solidified from lava erupted in a spreading zone between tectonic plates on the deep seafloor about 95 million years ago. Subsequent motions of the tectonic plates pushed this part of the seafloor to the surface by about 70 million years ago. —PHOTO COURTESY OF JOE CANN

A pile of lava pillows at about 12,000 feet depth in the mid-Atlantic spreading zone. An orange sea star attached to a pillow feeds on material in water that flows by. —PHOTO COURTESY OF DANIEL FORNARI, WOODS HOLE OCEANOGRAPHIC INSTITUTION

forming elongate, rounded shapes called *pillows*. The skin of a pillow acts like the walls of a pipe, and molten lava continues to flow inside. When that lava breaks through its pillow skin, a new pillow grows, and then another, and another, creating what can look like strings of gigantic sausages. When this happens for a long time, huge, thick piles of pillow lava build up. When geologists find pillow shapes in ancient basalt, they know the lava erupted underwater or flowed into water.

When magma erupts in deep seawater along the spreading zones between tectonic plates, the pressure from the weight of the water holds the magma's volatiles in and keeps the seawater from boiling. Explosive release of dissolved volatiles and steam explosions of heated seawater can only happen in shallow water.

Villarrica Volcano in the Andes Mountains of Chile, during a mild eruption in 1977. Within the historic record, Villarrica is the most active volcano in Chile. It lies above the subduction zone where the Nazca Plate plunges into the mantle beneath the South American Plate. Villarrica is close to the epicenter of the magnitude 8.8 earthquake of February 27, 2010, and even closer to the epicenter of the magnitude 9.5 earthquake of May 22, 1960, the most powerful earthquake ever recorded.

Can ERUPTIONS Be Predicted?

Can eruptions be predicted? The answer to this question depends on how the word *predict* is defined. If it means saying exactly when and where an eruption will occur and describing the style and size of that eruption, the answer is no. It is possible, though, to make a prediction that includes a big dose of "maybe," similar to how meteorologists predict the weather. The word *forecast* is probably a better description in both cases. With the weather, there are so many variables that affect the behavior of the atmosphere that a high probability of rain still doesn't tell you that you'll need to carry an umbrella if you want to stay dry. People who absolutely don't want to get wet take an umbrella. In the case of volcanoes, there are so many variables that affect the behavior of magma rising to the surface that people who absolutely don't want to be in the path of an eruption leave the area around a volcano when an eruption is forecast.

There are two ways to forecast a volcanic eruption. One method is based on the history of eruptions, and the other is based on current conditions, such as earthquake activity. To forecast based on history, geologists map a volcano's lava and tephra deposits to determine their size, meaning volume of magma erupted, and distribution, meaning land area affected by the eruption. Radioactive isotopes, like carbon-14, are used to determine the age of the deposits so that time-related patterns of eruption size and style can be projected forward to generate a forecast.

There are limitations to using the past record to forecast future eruptions. One is that some eruptions may not leave a record of lava or tephra. Small deposits can be eroded away, yet the eruption that produced them might have been powerful enough to threaten the safety of nearby people and property. Another limitation is that deposits from an eruption

63

may be completely buried, so they aren't exposed in outcrops for geologists to study. And, of course, if a brand-new volcano erupts, like Sunset Crater in Arizona and Paricutín in Mexico, there are no earlier deposits to study.

In spite of the limitations, one instance of using the past record to forecast the future eruption of a stratovolcano is an impressive success story. During the 1970s, U.S. Geological Survey geologists Dwight Crandell and Donal Mullineaux mapped and studied the prehistoric eruptive products of Mount St. Helens. In a report published in 1978 they wrote, "An eruption is likely to occur within the next hundred years, and perhaps even before the end of this century." That forecast was proved correct on May 18, 1980. The eruption actually announced its pending arrival two months earlier in the form of hundreds of earthquakes caused by magma rising up under the volcano.

Such earthquakes and related rumblings, used in the second forecast method, provide real-time warnings that a volcano may soon erupt. Magma can't sneak up through the crust without broadcasting its presence and path. It causes earthquakes as it shoulders rocks aside to create an upward pathway. As it gets close to the surface, volatiles begin to escape, rising through cracks in the crust and leaking out into the atmosphere. The ground surface above rising magma bulges upward and outward, like an inflating balloon, to make room for the new material that's being injected into the crust. The new magma may also change the electrical, magnetic, and gravitational properties of the surrounding crust.

All of these effects of magma rising into the crust can be measured continuously if enough people and equipment are available. Unfortunately, this isn't practical for all of Earth's volcanoes. Instead, only volcanoes that threaten people and property are watched 24/7. The most important tool in this monitoring is a seismometer, an instrument that measures earthquakes. It's true that many earthquakes are entirely unrelated to volcanoes headed toward an eruption. But when swarms of earthquakes rise up through a small area of the crust, magma is almost certainly on the move. Geologists may then want to start measuring other indicators of rising magma in an attempt to correctly forecast what's to come.

Fairly accurate forecasts are routine for Kilauea Volcano in Hawaii. And successes at Mount St. Helens in 1980 and at the Philippine volcano Pinatubo in 1991 helped reduce loss of life and property below what would have happened otherwise. Many countries now maintain volcano observatories to issue warnings of possible eruptions. The U.S. Geological Survey, in cooperation with various universities, maintains observatories for volcanoes in Hawaii, Alaska, the Cascades, Yellowstone, and the Long Valley region of California.

Scientists install monitoring equipment on the lava dome on Mount St. Helens in November 2005. Mount Rainier looms in the distance. —PHOTO COURTESY OF DAVE SHERROD, U.S. GEOLOGICAL SURVEY

At 14,410 feet, Mount Rainier forms a lovely yet ominous snow-draped backdrop, 35 miles southeast of Tacoma, Washington. As recently as 600 years ago, part of the volcano broke away and produced a landslide that flowed almost to Puget Sound, filling a river valley. Modern housing subdivisions between Tacoma and Rainier are built on this deposit. Many similar water-saturated slides from Rainier have occurred during the past 5,000 years, and the future will surely include more. —PHOTO COURTESY OF LYN TOPINKA, U.S. GEOLOGICAL SURVEY

Are VOLCANOES Our Friends or Enemies?

A friend of mine says, "An erupting volcano can ruin a perfectly good picnic." And, of course, he's right. In addition to the obvious hazards of hot lava, debris flows, steam, and tephra, eruptions may also trigger deadly floods by breaching crater lakes or melting a tall volcano's ice and snow. Some eruptions on islands and at undersea volcanoes near land create tsunamis, huge waves that are very destructive—and sometimes deadly when they wash up onto inhabited coastal areas. In 1883, a violent eruption of Krakatau Volcano between the Indonesian islands of Java and Sumatra produced a tsunami that killed nearly forty thousand people. No one died from lava or tephra, though. Over the past 1,000 years, at least several hundred thousand people have died because of volcanoes and their eruptions.

Tephra can be a big problem, not only causing disruption and destruction on the ground, but also presenting a hazard to airplanes. As it drifts downwind high in the atmosphere, far from the source volcano, a cloud of the fine gritty tephra called *ash* looks like a normal weather cloud. Some pilots have been caught in or mistakenly flown into ash clouds. Volcanic ash consists of tiny fragments of rocks and minerals that can sandblast the front windshield, reducing visibility. In addition, ash gets sucked into planes' engines. The temperature in the combustion chamber of a jet engine is so hot that it melts the ash. Then, toward the exhaust end of the engine, the new "magma" cools enough to solidify and clog up critical parts. In several cases, engines of jet aircraft have shut down when this happened. Fortunately, in each case the pilot was able to glide out of the ash cloud and eventually restart the engines for a safe landing. A worldwide warning system now advises aircraft away from ash clouds.

An unusual volcano-related disaster occurred one night in 1986, when the crater lake of Nyos Volcano, in Cameroon, Africa, suddenly burped out huge amounts of carbon dioxide that was dissolved in the water. The carbon dioxide originally came from magma below the lake. For some unknown reason, conditions suddenly changed, and the gas spewed out of the lake water in a giant version of what happens when the tab is popped on a warm can of carbonated cola that's been shaken. Carbon dioxide is denser than the atmosphere, so this invisible gas flowed silently downhill through villages near Nyos, suffocating about 1,700 sleeping people and 3,500 of their cattle.

Though there are significant hazards, not all eruptions are dangerous. Watching from a safe distance as a tame shield volcano, like Kilauea in Hawaii, erupts can be a fun outing. Still, no one should consider getting anywhere near the eruption of a silica-rich caldera-forming volcano, or even the relatively smaller eruptions of stratovolcanoes, such as Mount St. Helens. And even normally gentle Kilauea erupts violently when its molten rock mixes with water.

In spite of the dangers, millions of people live on and near volcanoes, and this number will probably rise as the world's population grows. One reason so many people live in the danger zone around volcanoes is because the farming is so good there. Volcanic ash contains phosphorus, potassium, and other important plant nutrients and makes incredibly rich and productive soil. Water circulating in soil leaches these and other nutrients from the ash, making them available to plants.

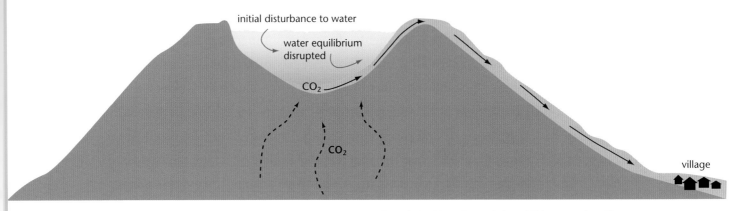

Because it is denser than the atmosphere, carbon dioxide from Lake Nyos flowed downhill into nearby villages.

Leaching is most effective when the surface area of contact between water and rock is greatest. Because a deposit of ash is made of many small pieces, each just a tiny fraction of an inch in size, the total area of contact between water and rock for a given volume of ash is huge. Water flowing through solid volcanic rock has a much smaller contact area, so it can't leach as many nutrients.

Mount Sundoro, an 8,000-foot-tall strato-volcano in Indonesia, has erupted many times during the past 200 years and will surely erupt again. The ash deposits around the volcano have created the rich agricultural land in the foreground.
—PHOTO COURTESY OF ROBERT TILLING, U.S. GEO-LOGICAL SURVEY

If you have a cube of rock that's 10 inches on a side, the total surface area is 600 square inches (100 square inches per side times 6 sides). When this hardworking geologist smashes the rock into lots of pieces, some bigger and some smaller, it turns out that the average size of a single piece is a 1-inch cube. Now the total surface area of exposed rock is 6,000 square inches (1,000 inch-sized cubes, each with a surface area of 6 square inches). If these two equal volumes of rock are saturated with groundwater, the water can dissolve more chemicals from the volume with the larger surface area. Plants grow better, therefore, on volcanic ash than on solid volcanic rock.

Whew! That's hard work. Where's a volcano when you need one?

MINING HEAT

Volcanoes and the shallow areas of their magma roots can be mined for heat. This resource—the abundant natural heat of planet Earth—is called *geothermal energy*. Magma and hot, recently solidified intrusive igneous rock heat up groundwater to 400 degrees Fahrenheit or more. Geothermal developers drill into these areas to reach the hot water. When the hot water rises to the surface through well pipes, it boils to steam that can spin a turbine to generate electricity. Unlike power plants that burn coal or natural gas to boil water into steam, those that use geothermal heat don't create carbon dioxide. And once the plant has been constructed and wells have been drilled into the hot water, the steam is free as long as it lasts. Most geothermal power plants around the world have been generating electricity for decades and are still going strong.

At temperatures below boiling (212 degrees Fahrenheit at sea level), Earth's natural hot water is used for heating buildings, swimming pools, and many other nonelectrical applications that would otherwise be likely to use natural gas or coal. Consider Iceland. This country sits over a mantle plume and is also astride the mid-Atlantic spreading zone, between the North American and

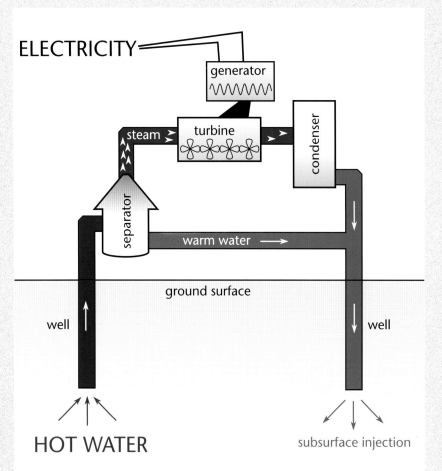

Using geothermal energy to generate electricity: Hot water (in the range of 400 to 600 degrees Fahrenheit) rises up the well on the left. At the surface, where the pressure is much lower than underground, water boils in the separator and the steam is routed to the turbine, which generates electricity. Steam from the turbine is condensed and combined with any water that didn't boil in the separator. This warm water is put down the well on the right, where it will be heated by hot rocks again.

Eurasian Plates. The country is made entirely of volcanoes, so it's perfect for taking advantage of Earth's heat. Almost all wells drilled in Iceland encounter warm or hot groundwater. This free energy is harnessed in several ways. For example, nearly all buildings are heated by running warm groundwater through radiators, and electricity is generated using high-temperature geothermal steam.

The geothermal electrical power plant at Coso, California, uses steam from several wells and can generate enough electricity for a town of about thirty-five thousand people.

The discovery well at the Coso geothermal area in California. The rocks behind the well are part of a rhyolite lava dome. The well is being tested to see how much steam it can produce. A well like this one can typically generate enough electricity for a town of about five thousand people.

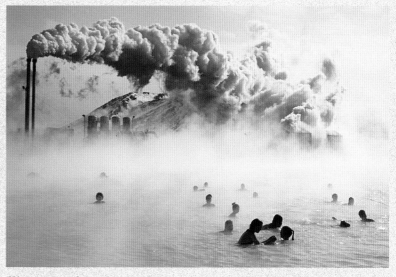

Warm water from the geothermal power plant in the background is fed into the Blue Lagoon, an open-air public swimming pool in Iceland. The water isn't put back underground because there's plenty of hot groundwater in Iceland. —PHOTO COURTESY OF ROBERT O. FOURNIER

During the long life span of a stratovolcano and the even longer lead-up to a caldera-forming eruption, most of the time is free of eruptions and safe for people going about their daily lives in the area. For volcano scientists concerned with hazards, the challenge is to closely monitor the day-to-day behavior of volcanoes so a warning can be issued to those living nearby when an eruption seems likely. When a volcano erupts and blankets an area with a new deposit of ash, it's definitely hazardous, and people need to get out of harm's way. But even though an eruption may kill the crops that are currently growing, it provides a rich source of nutrients for crops in future years.

FROM ASHES TO PRODUCTS

Volcanoes have inspired generations of poets, painters, and photographers. In addition, they also produce rock and ash—useful resources for making things. Lava flows and ash-flow tuffs are quarried for stone used in constructing buildings, bridges, roads, and other structures. Volcanic ash can be used to make pottery. In fact, coffee mugs were made from the 1980 Mount St. Helens ash.

The Azores of Portugal are volcanic islands in the Atlantic Ocean. In the city of Ponta Delgada, on São Miguel Island, sidewalks like these are made of blocks cut from local black basalt lava, decorated with mosaic patterns made of white limestone imported from mainland Portugal.

Magma and volcanoes have been part of Earth's long history from the very beginning, 4.55 billion years ago. From time to time along the way, various plants and animals have originated, flourished, and then disappeared. But a hot and restless inner Earth lives on, guaranteeing that humankind will live with volcanoes for the foreseeable future.

People will never be able to control volcanoes, although some have tried to divert or stop lava flows with bombs and Caterpillar tractors, with varying degrees of success. Some scientists even tried to trigger an eruption at Kilauea's Mauna Ulu vent in Hawaii, in part to prevent the volcano from building up more pressure to power a bigger eruption later on. Experiments like these can provide some temporary and local relief from damage due to eruptions, but Earth's internal heat machine is far more powerful than any countermeasure people can devise.

It seems that the most workable arrangement would be for us to keep trying to learn everything possible about volcanoes in order to adjust our lives and activities to minimize negative impacts from them. As we learn to better keep ourselves out of harm's way, we can still benefit from the resources volcanoes offer. We can harness their thermal energy to generate electricity and heat our buildings. We can grow crops on rich volcanic soils but avoid building homes and cities there. Instead, we can use volcanic rocks to build homes and other structures a safe distance away. When volcanoes are quiet, we can take advantage of recreational opportunities on their slopes. And at any time, we can find inspiration in their power and beauty.

COOLING DOWN

Forty years have slipped by since 1970, when I watched the Earth open up as molten rock pushed its way to the surface near Mauna Ulu on Kilauea's east slope. That introduction to volcanoes opened the first chapter of an exciting career I could only dream of back then. Since then, my studies have taken me to a variety of volcanoes on all continents except Antarctica, and more than a few volcanic islands. My goal has been to learn more about the behavior of these powerful critters, with the aim of figuring out how to harness some of their energy and other resources for human purposes while also learning how we might stay out of danger when they decide to violently vent.

There have been successes along the way, but there have also been missteps. I've lost a few colleagues whose devotion to volcano studies put them in harm's way at the wrong time. Three other volcanologist friends accidentally found themselves up to their knees in 2,000-degree-Fahrenheit lava flows at Kilauea and, rather incredibly, extracted themselves quickly enough to avoid permanent serious damage.

Over the years, I've suffered a few scratches and pesky burns—fortunately nothing substantial. But my seventy-year-old knees tell me it's time to let the next generation do the mountain climbing. I now experience the thrill of fieldwork secondhand, through collaborations with younger colleagues and by mentoring students whose energy and interest in the science are gratifying to share.

Supervolcanoes, calderas, stratovolcanoes, lava domes, cinder cones, maar volcanoes—all are fascinating to study. But whenever I reflect back on my career, my mind locks in on Kilauea, a shield volcano. The three years I worked at the Hawaii Volcano Observatory changed my life. Kilauea is where I first saw "live" lava. It was love at first sight, and that hot flame still burns. Unlike those other kinds of standoffish volcanoes, Kilauea usually lets you get up close and personal when she erupts, as I did when taking these photos.

Kilauea lava emerging from a pipelike tube spills into the Pacific Ocean along the south coast of Hawaii's Big Island.

This under-
ground river
of Kilauea lava
is so well
insulated by its
solid roof that it
flows down-
stream many
miles before
cooling enough
to solidify. The
geologist made
it safely across
the solidified
lava bridge!

This 3-foot-wide
pad of Kilauea
lava slowly oozes
forward over a
layer of cinders.
As new lava feeds
the lower part of
the leading edge,
the toe moves like
a reverse Caterpil-
lar tractor tread,
picking up cinders
that end up atop
the lava.

This 10-foot-tall bubbler on Kilauea is called a hornito, which means "little oven" in Spanish. This feature taps into an underlying deep pool of lava that has released just enough volatiles to break through the pool's crust.

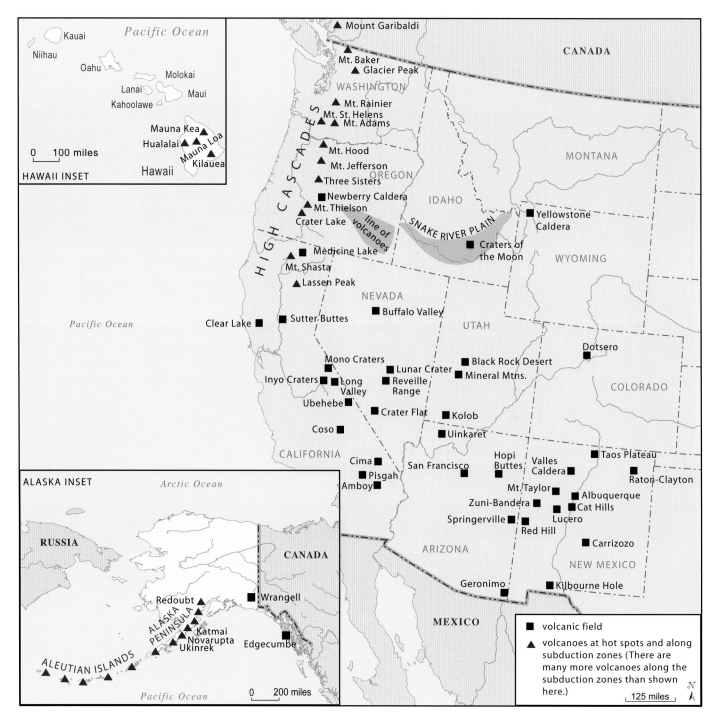

Young volcanoes and volcanic fields in the United States.

WHERE TO EXPLORE YOUNG VOLCANOES IN THE UNITED STATES

The following state-by-state list of volcanoes and volcanic fields includes many places discussed in the text of this book and also notes other volcanoes of interest. The list emphasizes volcanoes that are young enough to look like the kind of feature implied by the word *volcano*. Keep in mind, though, that volcanism has been a common geologic process throughout Earth's 4.55-billion-year history. It's just that most of the ancient volcanoes and their erupted products have been eroded down or entirely away—or have disappeared back into the mantle at subduction zones. For a comprehensive list of U.S. volcanoes no older than 5 million years, along with descriptions and directions on how to visit them, consult the book *Volcanoes of North America: The United States and Canada*, compiled by Charles Arthur Wood and Jürgen Kienle and published by Cambridge University Press.

ALASKA
Mount Edgecumbe Volcanic Field
Volcanoes of the Alaska Peninsula
Volcanoes along the entire length of the Aleutian Islands
Wrangell Volcanic Field

ARIZONA
Geronimo Volcanic Field
Hopi Buttes
San Francisco Volcanic Field
Springerville Volcanic Field
Uinkaret Volcanic Field

CALIFORNIA
Amboy Crater and Volcanic Field
Cima Volcanic Field
Clear Lake Volcanic Field
Coso Volcanic Field
Inyo Craters
Lassen Peak
Long Valley Caldera
Medicine Lake Caldera and surrounding volcanic field
Mono Craters
Pisgah Crater and Volcanic Field
Shasta, Mount
Sutter Buttes
Ubehebe Craters

COLORADO
Dotsero maar volcano

HAWAII
The entirety of the Hawaiian Islands

IDAHO

Snake River Plain, including Craters of the Moon National Monument

NEVADA

Buffalo Valley Volcanic Field

Crater Flat Volcanic Field

Lunar Crater Volcanic Field

Reveille Range Volcanic Field

NEW MEXICO

Albuquerque Volcanic Field

Carrizozo Volcanic Field

Cat Hills Volcanic Field

Kilbourne Hole maar volcano

Lucero Volcanic Field

Raton-Clayton Volcanic Field

Red Hill and Zuni Salt Lake maar volcanoes

Taos Plateau Volcanic Field

Taylor, Mount

Valles Caldera

Zuni-Bandera Volcanic Field

OREGON

Cascade Range: hundreds of small volcanoes and several large volcanic features including Crater Lake Caldera (Mount Mazama), Mount Hood, Mount Jefferson, Three Sisters, and Mount Thielson

Newberry Caldera and surrounding volcanic field

A zone of older volcanoes that extends east-southeast from Newberry Caldera to the Idaho state line, becoming progressively older to the east

UTAH

Black Rock Desert Volcanic Field

Kolob Volcanic Field

Mineral Mountains–Cove Fort Volcanic Field

WASHINGTON

Cascade Range (excluding the North Cascades): hundreds of small volcanoes and several large volcanic peaks, including Mount Adams, Mount Baker, Glacier Peak, Mount Rainier, and Mount St. Helens

WYOMING

Yellowstone Caldera

GLOSSARY

andesite. A volcanic rock in the range of about 52 to 63 percent silica. Andesite is more viscous than basalt but less viscous than dacite. Stratovolcanoes consist mostly of andesite.

ash, volcanic. Rock and mineral fragments smaller than 0.1 inch in diameter produced during a volcanic eruption.

ash-flow tuff. A rock deposit that forms from a mixture of ash and larger volcanic fragments that flowed down the flank of a volcano before coming to rest.

asthenosphere. The zone in the upper mantle, right below the lithosphere, that is hot and soft enough to slow earthquake waves, to flow in convection loops, and to be the source of much magma.

basalt. A volcanic rock in the range of about 48 to 52 percent silica. Basalt is the primary magma that forms when Earth's mantle begins to melt. Of the main types of magma, basalt is the least viscous and contains the least volatiles.

black smoker. A chimney-shaped vent on the seafloor along a spreading zone between tectonic plates, through which hot, mineral-rich water flows out into the sea.

calcium carbonate. The chemical description (one calcium atom, one carbon atom, and three oxygen atoms) of the mineral calcite. The common sedimentary rock limestone consists of calcite. Under high pressure and temperature, limestone is transformed into the metamorphic rock marble.

caldera. A large volcanic crater caused by collapse of the ground into the space vacated by rapidly erupted magma.

carapace breccia. A covering of fractured and tumbled volcanic rock that forms when the chilled and solidified outside of a lava dome or flow is pushed beyond its breaking point by a growing liquid core.

carbon dioxide. A gas made of one carbon atom and two oxygen atoms. Carbon dioxide is a normal part of Earth's atmosphere. It is also one of the primary volatile constituents in magma.

cinder, volcanic. A frothy volcanic fragment about 2 inches or somewhat larger in diameter. Cinders are produced when basalt and andesite lava fountains out of a volcano during an eruption. Synonymous with *scoria*.

cinder cone. A cone-shaped volcano made of cinders that formed when blobs of fountaining magma solidified during flight and fell to the ground around the erupting vent.

crater, volcanic. A closed depression that forms over an erupting volcanic vent.

crust. The uppermost few miles of Earth's rocky body, as defined by a relatively slow velocity for earthquake waves. It's also the brittle, flaky covering on my mom's apple pie.

dacite. A volcanic rock in the range of about 63 to 68 percent silica. Dacite is more viscous than andesite but less viscous than rhyolite.

debris avalanche, volcanic. A dry mixture of large and small rock fragments flowing down a steep volcano slope. Also refers to the deposit when it comes to rest.

dike, volcanic. A tabular (sheetlike) rock that cuts across the layering of rocks that surround it. A volcanic dike represents solidified magma that did not rise to the surface to erupt.

earthquake. A natural shaking of Earth that occurs when stress builds to the point that brittle rocks break.

epicenter. The location on Earth's surface directly above the point of origin of an earthquake.

feldspar. A group of silicate minerals that crystallize from all of the magma types. Feldspar in basalt is rich in calcium. Feldspar in the more silica-rich lava types is rich in sodium and potassium. Feldspar is the most common mineral in the Earth's crust.

flood basalt. The product of a brief, massive eruption of basalt magma that floods a region of hundreds of square miles with thousands of cubic miles of lava.

hot spot. A spot on Earth's surface where intense volcanism occurs because of heat from an underlying pipelike stream of magma (called a *mantle plume*) that rises within the mantle. Examples include the Yellowstone Caldera, Iceland, and the presently active part of the Hawaiian island chain.

igneous rock. A rock that forms by the solidification of molten rock. Igneous rocks that form beneath earth's surface are called intrusive. Common examples are granite and gabbro. Igneous rocks that form on Earth's surface are called extrusive, and these are the materials produced by volcanic eruptions.

lava. The name given to magma once it reaches Earth's surface. The name also applies to the solid rock that forms when liquid lava cools.

lava dome. A roughly dome-shaped volcanic mountain, most commonly made of dacite or rhyolite magma.

limestone. A calcium carbonate sedimentary rock that commonly forms on the seafloor.

lithosphere. The Earth's crust and the uppermost part of the mantle that together form a brittle zone on top of the asthenosphere. The Earth's tectonic plates are pieces of the lithosphere.

maar. A volcanic crater that forms when rising magma encounters shallow groundwater, triggering steam explosions that blast out the crater.

magma. Underground molten rock that contains dissolved gases (volatiles) and perhaps some crystals. When magma reaches Earth's surface, it's called *lava*.

mantle. The part of Earth between the core and crust. The mantle accounts for nearly 85 percent of Earth's volume.

mantle plume. A pipelike stream of magma that rises upward within the mantle and heats the base of the crust, creating a hot spot.

metamorphic rock. Any rock that is created from a preexisting rock whose minerals and appearance are altered because of changes in temperature and pressure.

mineral. A naturally occurring solid substance that has a characteristic chemical composition and internal structure of its atoms.

mineral salts. Chemical constituents dissolved in water.

olivine. An iron- and magnesium-rich silicate mineral that's commonly present in basalt and other low-silica volcanic rocks.

pillow lava. Interconnected pillow-shaped bodies of lava that form when a lava flow enters water but doesn't mix with the water well enough to result in steam explosions. When they pile up, pillows look like gigantic strings of sausages stacked up on each other.

plate tectonics. A theory that describes the relative motion of pieces of Earth's outermost brittle shell of rock, the lithosphere.

pumice. A spongelike rhyolite or dacite rock filled with air bubbles that's so light it can float on water.

pyroxene. A calcium-, iron-, and magnesium-rich silicate mineral commonly present in basalt and andesite.

rhyolite. A volcanic rock in the general range of 68 to 77 percent silica. Molten rhyolite is the most viscous and volatile-rich of the common magma types. Most caldera-forming eruptions are of rhyolite.

sedimentary rock. A layered rock that consists of material eroded from other rocks or a chemical deposit from evaporating water rich in minerals.

shield volcano. A basalt volcano characterized by a broad profile of gently sloping flanks. Hawaii's Mauna Loa is a classic shield volcano.

silica. A substance composed of one atom of the element silicon linked to two atoms of oxygen. When geologists speak of silica content, they are referring to the amount of the element silicon in an igneous rock. Silica also occurs as a variety of minerals.

silicate mineral. A mineral whose main building blocks are like pyramids (one silicon atom surrounded by four oxygen atoms) connected by atoms of iron, magnesium, calcium, sodium, or potassium, and other metallic elements.

spreading zone. The area between two of Earth's tectonic plates that are moving away from each other.

stratovolcano. A tall, upward-steepening volcano that consists mostly of andesite. Stratovolcanoes commonly form above subduction zones.

subduction zone. A boundary between two of Earth's tectonic plates that are colliding with each other, with one plate plunging down into the mantle beneath the other plate.

supervolcano. The largest and most violent kind of volcano known. Examples are Toba in Sumatra and Yellowstone in the United States. No supervolcano has erupted during recorded historic time. If such an eruption occurs in the future, it will cause worldwide climate effects.

tectonic plate. A piece of Earth's lithosphere that moves relative to other tectonic plates.

tephra. A term describing all volcanic fragments formed during violent explosive eruptions.

transform fault. A boundary between two tectonic plates that are sliding sideways past one another.

tremor, volcanic. A low-level shaking of Earth due to volcanic forces. They can last anywhere from minutes to several hours. They are commonly caused by the underground flow of magma, and maybe also volatile gases escaping from magma. Volcanic tremors are similar to the constant shaking caused by the long, drawn-out bass note of a loud music system. Volcanic tremors are an indicator that an eruption may happen soon.

tsunami. A large ocean wave produced by a seafloor earthquake, a large landslide into the sea, or a seafloor volcanic eruption. Popularly called a "tidal wave," but a tsunami is not related to tides.

vent, volcanic. An opening where magma erupts to Earth's surface.

viscosity. A measure of the resistance of a fluid to flow. Fluids considered runny, like water, have low viscosity. Those considered thick, like honey, have high viscosity. Among magmas, basalt is considered runny and rhyolite is considered thick. Andesite and dacite are intermediate.

volatiles. A substance dissolved in magma that escapes into the atmosphere as a gas when the magma rises near or to Earth's surface. Water, carbon dioxide, and various sulfurous compounds are the most common volatiles in magma.

RESOURCES

BOOKS ABOUT VOLCANOES

Decker, Robert, and Barbara Decker. 1997. *Volcanoes*. Third Edition. W. H. Freeman.

Fisher, Richard V., and Grant Heiken. 1998. *Volcanoes: Crucibles of Change*. Princeton University Press.

Harris, Stephen L. 2005. *Fire Mountains of the West: The Cascade and Mono Lake Volcanoes*. Third Edition. Mountain Press Publishing Company.

Krafft, Maurice. 1993. *Volcanoes: Fire from the Earth*. Harry N. Abrams.

Simkin, Tom, and Lee Siebert. 1994. *Volcanoes of the World*. Second Edition. Geoscience Press.

VOLCANO WEBSITES

http://mineralsciences.si.edu/tdpmap (Smithsonian Institution interactive geologic map that shows Earth's active volcanoes)

www.volcano.si.edu (The Smithsonian Institution's Global Volcanism Program website)

www.volcano.si.edu/reports/usgs (Weekly updated global volcanic activity reports, compiled by the Smithsonian Institution and the U.S. Geological Survey)

volcanoes.usgs.gov/lvo (USGS Long Valley Volcano Observatory for Long Valley Caldera, California, and other nearby volcanoes)

www.geo.mtu.edu/volcanoes (Michigan Technological University volcanoes website)

www.photovolcanica.com (Volcano photographs and information by Dr. Richard Roscoe)

http://hvo.wr.usgs.gov (USGS Hawaiian Volcano Observatory)

www.avo.alaska.edu (USGS and University of Alaska Volcano Observatory)

http://vulcan.wr.usgs.gov/ (USGS Cascades Volcano Observatory)

http://gsc.nrcan.gc.ca/volcanoes/index_e.php (Geological Survey of Canada, Volcanoes of Canada website)

http://volcanoheaven.tumblr.com (Some of the world's most artful and dramatic volcano photos, by Donna and Steve O'Meara)

INDEX

air, 6. *See also* atmosphere
Alae Crater, 4
Alaska, 16, 24, 26, 38, 44, 46, 59
Aleutian Islands, 16, 24, 38
Aleutian Trench, 24
Andes, 17, 62
andesite, 28, 29, 38, 39
Aniakchak Caldera, 52
Antarctica, 39
Arizona, 21, 25, 32, 33, 45, 64
ash, 8, 26, 27, 39, 67, 68, 69, 72
ashfall, 49, 55
ash-flow tuff, 48, 50, 72
asthenosphere, 15
Atlantic Ocean, 18, 61
atmosphere, 6, 8, 26, 36
Azores, 72

basalt, 27, 28–30, 72; cinder cones of,
    31–33; floods of, 35–37
Big Island, 1, 21, 75
black smoker, 19
Blue Lagoon (Iceland), 71
breccia, 44, 45

calcium, 28
calcium carbonate, 12
calderas, 35, 46–55
California, 20, 43, 46, 51, 71
Cameroon, 68
carapace breccia, 44, 45, 46
carbon-14, 63
carbon dioxide, 68
Caribbean Sea, 9

Carrizo Plain, 20
Cascade Range, 17. *See also* Rainier,
    Mount; St. Helens, Mount
Chain of Craters Road, vi
Chicxulub, 36
Chili, 62
cinder cones, 31–33
cinders, 31
collision zone, 16
Columbia Plateau flood basalt, 36, 37
composite volcanoes. *See* stratovolcanoes
conduction, 11, 12
continental plates, 16
convection, 11, 12
core (Earth's), 6, 7, 16
corn casts, 33
Coso Volcanic Field, 43, 46, 71
coulee, 46
Crater Elegante, 58
Crater Lake Caldera, 47, 48, 51, 52
crust (Earth's), 6, 7, 13, 15, 16, 17
curtain of fire, 3

dacite, 28, 29, 43, 48
Dead Sea, 21
decay, 9
Deccan flood basalt, 36
density, 6, 11
dikes, 35, 37
domes, lava, 9, 42–46

Earth: age of, 5; formation of, 5; heat in,
    5, 6, 7, 9, 10–12, 16, 70–71; internal
    structure of, 6

earthquakes, 2, 3, 13, 15, 64
Eifel District, 58
Elden Mountain, 45
electricity, 9, 70–71
endogenous, 43–44, 46
Erebus, Mount, 39
eruption forecasting, 63–65
Everest, Mount, 18
exogenous, 43, 45, 46

faults, 20, 21
feldspar, 39
Flagstaff, 25, 32, 45
flood basalt, 35–37
forecasting, 63–65
fountaining stage, 31
Fuji, Mount, 38
fumes, 9, 26

gases, 27, 30. *See also* volatiles
geothermal energy, 70–71
glass, volcanic, 1, 60
groundwater, 12, 57–59, 69
Guatemala, 46

half life, 10
Hawaii, 1–3, 21, 22, 23, 24, 34, 60, 74–77
Hawaiian Volcano Observatory, 1, 74
heat conduction, 11, 12
heat convection, 11, 12
Himalayas, 17
Hood, Mount, 38
hornito, 77
hot spot, 12, 16, 21
hot springs, 12, 70–71
Hualalai Volcano, 21

Iceland, 18, 70–71
igneous rocks, 7

India, 17, 36
Indonesia, 67, 69
iron, 7, 28
isotopes, 9, 10, 63

Japan, 16
Juan de Fuca Plate, 14, 19

Kilauea Volcano, 1–3, 21, 22, 56, 74–77;
    crater of, 4; eruptions of, 3, 64, 68;
    lava of, vi, 4, 22–23
Krakatau Volcano, 67
Kuril Islands, 8

landslides, 39, 66
lava, 8; of ocean floor, 18, 19. *See also*
    basalt; domes, lava
lava lakes, 22–23, 39
lithosphere, 15
Loihi Volcano, 21
Long Valley Caldera, 49, 51

maar volcanoes, 58–59
magma, 7, 8; changes in, 28; formation
    of, 17; tremors caused by, 2; types of,
    27; and water, 57–59
magnesium, 28
mantle, 6, 7, 11, 13, 15, 16, 25
mantle plume, 11, 12, 16, 21, 35
Mariana Trench, 14, 16
Mauna Loa, 21, 34
Mauna Ulu, vi, 2, 22–23, 73. *See also*
    Kilauea
Mazama, Mount, 51. *See also* Crater Lake
melting, 17
metamorphic rocks, 7
meteorite impact, 36
Mexico, 33, 58
Moho, 15

Montserrat, 9, 46

Native Americans, 21, 25, 33
New Mexico, 50, 53
New Zealand, 54
nickel, 7
North American Plate, 14, 20, 25
Novarupta, 44, 46
Nyos Volcano, 68

observatories, 65
oceans, 6, 18; trenches of 16
ocean-floor plates, 13, 16, 19
olivine, 28
Oman, 61
Oregon, 36, 37, 47
Oruanui, 54

Pacific Ocean, 16, 21, 33, 38, 56, 60, 75
Pacific Plate, 14, 16, 19, 20, 21
Paricutín, 33, 64
Philippine Plate, 14, 16, 64
pillow lava, 60–61
Pinacate Volcanic Field, 58
Pinatubo Volcano, 64
plate tectonics, 13, 14, 15, 16, 18, 19,
    21, 22
Ponta Delgada, 72
Portugal, 72
potassium, 7
predictions, 63–65
pressure, 7, 10, 18, 21, 27, 30, 61
pumice, 27, 49
pyroclastic eruptions, 46–55
pyroxene, 28

radioactivity, 9, 10
Rainier, Mount, 65, 66
Redoubt Volcano, 26

rhyolite, 28, 29, 43, 48
rift zones, 35
rock: melting of, 17, 27; types of, 7
Russia, 8

salts, mineral, 12
San Andreas Fault, 20
San Francisco Volcanic Field, 32–33
Santiaguito, 46
Sarychev Volcano, 8
sedimentary rocks, 7
seismic activity, 2, 64
seismometer, 64
shield volcanoes, 34–35
silica, 12, 28–29
silicate mineral, 7
sinter, 12
sodium, 7
soils, 68, 69
Soufriere Hills Volcano, 9, 46
South American Plate, 14, 62
SP Crater, 32
spreading zones, 16, 18, 19, 70
springs, hot, 12
steam, explosions of, 26, 56, 57–59, 60
St. Helens, Mount, 40–42, 46, 49, 64,
    65, 68
stratovolcanoes, 26, 38–42
subduction zones, 13, 16, 17
Sumatra, 54
Sundoro Volcano, 69
Sunset Crater, 21, 25, 33, 64
supervolcanoes, 54

Taupo Lake, 54
tephra, 27, 39, 43, 46, 48, 67
thermal equilibrium, 10
Toba Volcano, 54
transform faults, 20, 21

travertine, 12
tremors, 2, 3
trench, 16
tsunami, 67

Ukinrek Volcano, 59
uranium, 9

Valles Caldera, 50, 53
Valley of Ten Thousand Smokes, 44, 46
vesicles, 31
Villarrica Volcano, 62
viscosity, 27, 30
volatiles, 27, 29, 30, 40, 43, 49, 57, 61, 64

volcanic explosivity index, 54
volcanic fields, 33
volcanic glass, 1, 60
volcanoes: island chains of, 21, 24; location of, 13–25, 14, 78; number of, 8; types of, 27–55

Washington, 36, 40, 66
water, 6, 17, 57–61
West Mata Volcano, 60
Wizard Island, 47

Yellowstone, 25, 54, 55

The author sits atop a prehistoric cinder cone to enjoy the view of the Mauna Ulu vent in full eruption in 1969. It doesn't get much more exciting than this!
—PHOTO COURTESY OF DON SWANSON, U.S. GEOLOGICAL SURVEY

ABOUT THE AUTHOR

Wendell A. Duffield received a BA in geology from Carleton College, Northfield, Minnesota, in 1963, and MS and PhD degrees in geology from Stanford University in 1965 and 1967. Subsequently, he was a scientist in volcano research for more than forty years, the first thirty as an employee of the United States Geological Survey, and since 1997 as an adjunct professor of geology at Northern Arizona University in Flagstaff. He has contributed more than 150 titles to peer-reviewed research literature.

Other volcano-related books by Wendell A. Duffield

NONFICTION

Chasing Lava: A Geologist's Adventures at the Hawaiian Volcano Observatory

Volcanoes of Northern Arizona: Sleeping Giants of the Grand Canyon Region

FICTION

When Pele Stirs: A Volcanic Tale of Hawaii, Hemp, and High-Jinks

Yucca Mountain Dirty Bomb